WITHDRAWN

THE MOTIVE FOR METAPHOR

In Honor of Samuel French Morse

1983

The Motive for Metaphor

Essays on Modern Poetry

EDITED BY

Francis C. Blessington

AND

Guy Rotella

Northeastern University Press · Boston

Designer, Richard C. Bartlett

Northeastern University Press

Library of Congress Cataloging in Publication Data

The Motive for metaphor
    Includes index.
    1. American poetry—20th century—History and criticism—Addresses, essays, lectures. 2. Stevens, Wallace, 1879–1955—Criticism and interpretation—Addresses, essays, lectures. 3. Criticism—Addresses, essays, lectures. 4. Morse, Samuel French, 1916– —criticism and interpretation—Addresses, essays, lectures. 5. American poetry—20th century. I. Morse, Samuel French, 1916– . II. Blessington, Francis C., 1942– . III. Rotella, Guy L., 1947– .
PS323.5.M67   1983   811'.52'09   82-22280
                ISBN 0-930350-38-3

Acknowledgments

The editors would like to acknowledge the aid and encouragement of the following members of the Northeastern University English Department, both faculty and staff: Professors Gordon Pruett, Earl Harbert, and Kinley Roby, and Ms. Ava Baker and Ms. Lori Maika. We would also like to thank Professor Ann Taylor Blessington of Salem State College for her helpful suggestions and William A. Frohlich and Deborah Kops of Northeastern University Press for their continued interest in this project.

We wish to thank the following for permission to reprint material:

Atheneum Publishers, "Keeping Things Whole" from *Selected Poems*. Copyright ©1964, 1980 by Mark Strand.

Kenneth Burke, "Creation Myth" from *Collected Poems*. Copyright ©1968 by The University of California Press.

Clive E. Driver, excerpts from the unpublished writings of Marianne Moore. Copyright © 1983 by Clive E. Driver, Literary Executor of the Estate of Marianne C. Moore.

Alan Dugan, "On Looking for Models" from *Poems 4*, Little, Brown and Company. Copyright ©1974 by Alan Dugan.

The Ecco Press, "Homeric Simile" from *Praise*, by Robert Hass. Copyright © 1979 by The Ecco Press.

Faber and Faber Publishers, "Home Is So Sad" and excerpts from "The Whitsun Weddings," "Naturally the Foundation Will Bear Your Expenses," "An Arundel Tomb," "Self's the Man," and "Toads Revisited," from *The Whitsun Weddings*. Copyright ©1964 by Philip Larkin. Excerpts from "I see a girl dragged by the wrists" from *The North Ship*. Copyright © 1966 by Philip Larkin.

Farrar, Straus and Giroux, Inc., excerpts from "Cut Grass," "Forget What Did," "Posterity," and "To the Sea" from *High Windows*. Copyright © 1974 by Philip Larkin.

David Fisher, "The Bear" from *Teachings*, Ross/Backroads Books. Copyright ©1978 by David Fisher.

Harper & Row, Publishers, Inc., "A Late Guest at the Stevens Party" from *A Glass Face in the Rain*. Copyright ©1982 by William Stafford.

Acknowledgments

Holt, Rinehart and Winston, excerpts from "Snow" and "Out, Out—" from *The Poetry of Robert Frost.* Copyright ©1969 by Holt, Rinehart and Winston.

Michael Gibson, for the estate of W. W. Gibson, excerpts from "The Golden Room," from *the Golden Room and Other Poems,* Macmillan Publishing Company. Copyright ©1928 by Wilfred Gibson.

Indiana University Press, "This is a Wonderful Poem" by David Wagoner, from *Collected Poems, 1956–1976.* Copyright ©1976 by Indiana University Press.

Alfred A. Knopf, Inc., excerpts from "The Motive for Metaphor," "The Man Whose Pharynx Was Bad," "The Man With the Blue Guitar," "The Mechanical Optimist," "A Thought Revolved," "Lions in Sweden," "Like Decorations in a Nigger Cemetery," "Of Hartford in a Purple Light," "The Common Life," "The Poems of Our Climate," "Anything is Beautiful If You Say It Is," "The Glass of Water," "The Latest Freed Man," "Notes toward a Supreme Fiction," "A Completely New Set of Objects," "Debris of Life and Mind," "The Plain Sense of Things," "How to Live. What to Do," "Extracts from Addresses to the Academy of Fine Ideas," "Some Friends from Pascagoula," "Ghosts as Cocoons," "The Pleasures of Merely Circulating," "Connoisseur of Chaos," "The Bed of Old John Zeller," "Credences of Summer," "The Auroras of Autumn," "Long and Sluggish Lines," "Prologues to What Is Possible," "To an Old Philosopher in Rome," and "The Planet on the Table" from *The Collected Poems of Wallace Stevens.* Copyright ©1954 by Wallace Stevens. Exerpts from "Adagia," "Williams," "A Clear Day and No Memories," "Recitation After Dinner," "Five Grotesque Pieces," "As You Leave the Room," and "On the Way to the Bus" from *Opus Posthumous,* edited by Samual French Morse. Copyright ©1957 by Elsie Stevens and Holly Stevens. Excerpts from Wallace Stevens' letters from *Letters of Wallace Stevens,* edited by Holly Stevens. Copyright ©1966 by Holly Stevens. Excerpts from *The Necessary Angel.* Copyright ©1951 by Wallace Stevens.

Liveright Publishing Corporation, "The Whipping" from *Angle of Ascent: New and Selected Poems.* Copyright ©1975, 1972, 1970, 1966 by Robert Hayden.

Macmillan Publishing Company, "Roses Only" and "Those Various Scalpels" from *Collected Poems.* Copyright ©1935 by Marianne Moore, renewed ©1963 by Marianne Moore and T. S. Eliot. Excerpts from "A Dialogue of Self and Soul," "Vacillation," "The Statesman's Holiday," and "The Apparitions," by William Butler Yeats. Copyright © 1933 by Macmillan Publishing Co., renewed ©1961 by Bertha Georgie Yeats; copyright ©1940 by Georgie Yeats, renewed ©1968 by Bertha Georgie Yeats, Michael Yeats, and Anne Yeats.

The Marvell Press (England), excerpts from "Latest Face," "Reasons for Attendance," and "Spring" from *The Less Deceived* by Philip Larkin. Copyright © 1955 by The Marvell Press.

New Directions, "The Rose" and "Portrait of a Lady" from *Collected Earlier Poems* by William Carlos Williams. Copyright ©1938 by New Directions.

Penguin Books Ltd., "Five Men" by Zbigniew Herbert, from *Selected Poems.* Translation copyright ©1968 by Czeslaw Milosz and Peter Dale Scott.

Contents

ROBERT PENN WARREN
Remark for Historians (*poem*)
· *xi* ·

Preface
· *xiii* ·

PART ONE
Wallace Stevens
· *1* ·

WILLIAM STAFFORD
A Late Guest at the Stevens Party (*poem*)
· *3* ·

SAMUEL FRENCH MORSE
A Sense of the Place
· *4* ·

FRANK DOGGETT AND DOROTHY EMERSON
About Stevens' Comments on Several Poems
· *26* ·

PETER BRAZEAU
"Hepped on Family Ties":
Wallace Stevens in the 1940s
· *37* ·

ROBERT BUTTEL
The Incandescence of Old Age:
Yeats and Stevens in Their Late Poems
· *48* ·

Contents

PART TWO
Other Modern Poets
· 61 ·

RICHARD EBERHART
Rain (*poem*)
· 63 ·

BONNIE COSTELLO
" 'Polished Garlands' of Agreeing Difference":
William Carlos Williams and Marianne Moore,
an Exchange
· 64 ·

JOHN F. SEARS
The Subversive Performer
in Frost's "Snow" and "Out, Out—"
· 82 ·

FRANCIS C. BLESSINGTON
"An Old-Type *Natural* Fouled-Up Guy":
The Conflicting Voice in Philip Larkin
· 93 ·

PART THREE
Some Remarks on Poetry and Criticism
· 109 ·

HOWARD BAKER
Salvage (*poem*)
· 111 ·

ROY HARVEY PEARCE
Poetry and Progress, Criticism and Culmination:
A Cautionary Tale
· 112 ·

WILLIAM MEREDITH
Reasons for Poetry and the Reason for Criticism
· 124 ·

Contents

PART FOUR
Samuel French Morse
· *145* ·

WILLIAM BRONK
Backtrack into the Swamp (*poem*)
· *147* ·

GUY ROTELLA
"A Certain Doubleness":
The Poetry of Samuel French Morse
· *148* ·

SAMUEL FRENCH MORSE
From "Beach Glass" (*poem*)
· *167* ·

A Candle for Advent (*poem*)
· *168* ·

The Contributors
· *169* ·

Index
· *171* ·

ROBERT PENN WARREN

Remark for Historians

Only Truth is deep as the ocean,
Where green, gold, and blue lights glow,
Dappling total dark where the slimed historian
Makes shine the natural light in his brow.

And still as the ocean depth is Truth
Where horned, slick monsters yet undefined
By science, with suck-plates, arms weaving, and tooth,
Prey on their, or monsters of other, kind.

But do not forget how glitter and glory,
From galley and round-ship to liner and dreadnought,
Have moved on the uncertain surface — and their story
Is often as dim as the depth they, feckless, sought.

Yes, we live for Truth, but what man has been
In its depth and lived to describe that bourn?
And all we know is its sunlit sheen
Or the wind-ripped medium where great waves mourn.

Preface

"The real is only the base. But it is the base."
Wallace Stevens, "Adagia"[1]

A. Walton Litz noted that the poetry of Wallace Stevens is "rich in its involvement with the particulars of time and place."[2] The critics in this book see modern poetry in much the same way. To them it is not only an expression of form but a representation of reality. The tension between that reality and poetry is, for them, central to its meaning. Viewed in this way, their criticism is an aspect of what Alfred North Whitehead saw as the most important problem in modern thinking: the Cartesian split between the observing self and its surrounding reality. As a result, they examine the relationship between object and word, content and form, matter and mind, real and ideal, objective and subjective. In short, they express a humanistic attitude toward literature that views it as a comment on life, a view once more widely held, but now not universally accepted.

The editors solicited these essays and poems from associates of Samuel French Morse to honor his retirement from teaching at Northeastern University. A poet and an authority on Wallace Stevens, Morse shares their humanistic view of literature. Stevens too shared this attitude. No matter how rootless his poetry appeared, Stevens believed that a grounding was necessary. As Morse remarks:

> "The Comedian as the letter C" had spelled out the consequences of confusing fancy with imagination and the error of assuming that either imagination or reality by itself was sufficient to live by. The poet was, after all, a man with a monocle: one eye naked to reality, one eye looking at the world imaginatively.[3]

In Stevens' own words, "in poetry at least the imagination must not detach itself from reality."[4] The motive for metaphor, he says in the poem by that name, is to heighten experience, to represent it imaginatively, but not to cancel it. In that poem, the imagination transforms, yet the poem ends with the reality that the imagination began by working on

> The ruddy temper, the hammer
> Of red and blue, the hard sound —
> Steel against intimation — the sharp flash,
> The vital, arrogant, fatal, dominant X.[5]

The first three divisions of this book represent the areas of Morse's scholarly interest and work: Wallace Stevens, other modern poets, and the relationship of poetry to criticism. A closing section analyzes Morse's own poetry. All the essays acknowledge the "dominant X," the importance of the real world, as part of the motive for metaphor. It would not be claiming too much to say that they defend reality's place in the poetic imagination. Some defend it directly and truculently; others, indirectly and subtly.

In Part I, "Wallace Stevens," Morse reveals a geographical basis for Stevens' poetry in his adopted hometown of Hartford, Connecticut. Frank Doggett and Dorothy Emerson expose Stevens' poetry to the colder reality of his prose comments. Peter Brazeau shows the poetic results of Stevens' interest in his genealogy. Robert Buttel contrasts Stevens and Yeats in their responses to the nearness of death.

The essays in Part II deal with other modern poets. Bonnie Costello draws subtle and opposing differences between the work of William Carlos Williams and that of Marianne Moore, and Francis C. Blessington analyzes the conflicts in Philip Larkin's poetic voice, as all three poets make, or refuse to make, their compromises with reality. Robert Frost's imaginative playing with his realistic settings and characters is the subject of John F. Sears's essay, which closes the section.

In the third part, "Some Remarks on Poetry and Criticism," one critic and one poet assess the current relationship between the reality of poetry and the imaginative act of criticism. Both argue for the acceptance of literature as a comment on life in its broadest and deepest sense. Roy Harvey Pearce finds some contemporary criticism lacking in respect for the individuality and the uniqueness of the poetic experience, while William Meredith asks the reader of modern poetry for greater breadth of understanding and broader sympathies.

In the closing essay, Guy Rotella shows Morse's poetry to be a shaping and an inclusion of the particulars of experience and to be the result of the clash between subjective and objective realities.

The essayists, the contributing poets, and Samuel French Morse would agree, we think, with Stevens' conviction that "it is life that we are trying to get in Poetry."[6]

Francis C. Blessington
Guy Rotella

NOTES

1. *Opus Posthumous,* ed. Samuel French Morse (New York: Knopf, 1957), p. 160.
2. *Harvard Guide to Contemporary American Writing,* ed. Daniel Hoffman (Cambridge: Harvard Univ. Press, 1979), p. 75.
3. *Wallace Stevens: Poetry as Life* (New York: Pegasus, 1970), p. 137.
4. *Opus Posthumous,* p. 161.
5. *The Collected Poems of Wallace Stevens* (New York: Knopf, 1954), p. 288.
6. *Opus Posthumous,* p. 158.

PART ONE

Wallace Stevens

WILLIAM STAFFORD

A Late Guest at the Stevens Party

I guess I thought it was music—that sound
at the party; they had the moon, that sort of old
light only the rich—or the desperate poor—
can clutch. I hid my shadow inside me
and stood by the door, realizing in a flood
that their terrace when I knocked would suddenly stop.

I knocked. In the long instant that followed
their house paled into glass and I was
a mirror they heard come into place
around them. It wasn't music. They froze.
All that they thought they had, they had to
give back in one glance when my shadow leaped.

Revelers, I'm sorry: I have to knock
in order to know if it really is music.

A Sense of the Place

"Life is an affair of people not of places. But for me
life is an affair of places and that is the trouble."
—Wallace Stevens, "Adagia"

In March 1954, the editors of *The Trinity Review*, the undergraduate
literary magazine at Trinity College, were putting to bed a *Festschrift* to
celebrate, albeit a few months early, the seventy-fifth birthday of
Wallace Stevens. It was a great occasion. Almost everyone who had been
asked to join the festivities had accepted. Poems had come from ten
poets, including Archibald MacLeish, Richard Wilbur, John Malcolm
Brinnin, and Richard Eberhart. Alfred A. Knopf, T. S. Eliot, Marianne
Moore, and Conrad Aiken were some of those who had sent tributes.
William Carlos Williams, Alfred Kreymborg, Louise Bogan, John L.
Sweeney, Cudworth Flint, and ten others had sent appreciative essays
written with an apt sense of the moment; and Arthur Berger had sent the
first page of his orchestral score "Ideas of Order." Stevens contributed
"The Rock," which had not been published previously in America, and
a new poem, "Not Ideas about the Thing but the Thing Itself," which
became the tailpiece of his *Collected Poems*, published on October 1,
the day before his birthday. Had we known that Stevens had confessed
to liking "Rhine wine, blue grapes, [and] good cheese" as much as he
liked "supreme fiction," there might also have been a proper picnic
under the campus elms. At any rate, in a letter written a week or two
after the *Festschrift* appeared, Stevens commented to Babette Deutsch:

> The *Trinity Review* is like a very rich chocolate cake. It
> would have been quite possible for me to sit down and devour
> the whole thing but I took a little of it here and there and then
> put it away. I don't suppose that you will believe that . . . but
> so help me God.[1]

The Stevens issue of *Trinity Review* has long been a collector's item. Twenty-five years later, 1979 marked another occasion for tributes; I only wish that Wallace Stevens had lived to celebrate his hundredth birthday, like his good friend of *Harvard Advocate* days, Murray Seasongood, who continued to work in his office up to—and probably after—his own centenary in 1978. What Stevens might have had to say would have been worth hearing in the light of his remarks about his seventy-fifth birthday. He told one friend:

> . . . although I have not paid the slightest attention to birthdays heretofore, I do feel a certain amount of interest in this one because it at least marks the beginning of the last quarter. By the time I am 100 I won't know what a birthday is. Possibly I am more fortunate than most people because I have really nothing whatever wrong with me except that I never made that million dollars that I started out to make. While this is a tremendous drawback, especially as the time for people to go to Florida rolls around, still there are compensations. Thus, I can sit at home and listen to WQXR. I have no plans that involve any change.
>
> (L, p. 846)

A few months earlier, recalling a refusal "to attend a celebration of the 80th birthday of Robert Frost," he had written to another friend:

> Frost is greatly admired by many people. I do not know his work well enough to be either impressed or unimpressed. When I visited the rare book library at Harvard some years ago the first thing I saw was his bust. His work is full (or said to be full) of humanity. I suppose I shall never be eighty no matter how old I become.
>
> (L, p. 825)

After making allowance for the malice that was part of the "ferocious" egoism of poets, one can be certain that he must also have meant that he expected to continue at the office and to enjoy "mere being"—occupations that would have kept him in Hartford, where he could "sit still to discover the world" and where "An evening's thought" might continue to be "like a day of clear weather."

I

Hartford has seldom evoked great praises from the writers we identify with it, at least in the works for which we remember them. Still, Mark Twain found it "the best built and handsomest town" he had ever seen, as congenial a place for work in winter as Elmira was in summer. Sinclair Lewis, however, after less than two weeks' residence, thought Hartford had "no virtues except that one can live in a lordly manner on not very much money, and that though it's quiet for work, it's also only three hours from N.Y."[2]

The fort that the seventeenth-century Dutch settlers established at the mouth of the river once called the Meandering Swine was, of course, more than three hours from New Amsterdam; the early settlers seem to have left no noteworthy literary account of the spot. Thomas Hooker, who arrived in 1636, was no local colorist either, although he was said to have made the local freemen "very jealous of their liberties"; Hooker gave the settlement its present name, from the English birthplace of his companion, Samuel Stone. The Hartford Wits, a century and a half later, regarded the material world with greater tolerance; imbued with rationalism and committed to ideas of order identifiable with affluence, they were admirably representative of the conservative values we now consider appropriate to the insurance capital of the world. If they did not altogether neglect "landskip" in their writings, their temper was Augustan rather than Romantic, and their literary pose was public, occasional, or satiric. David Humphreys composed a "Sonnet . . . Addressed To My Friends At Yale College, On My Leaving Them To Join The Army," which could have provided Wordsworth with as good an example of what he tactfully called "prosaisms" in his *Preface* as Gray's "Sonnet on the Death of Richard West." But New Haven was hardly Hartford—although it was Connecticut. Joel Barlow, in what may well have been his last poem, had his blackbird and his winter; but his couplets constituted "Advice to a Raven in Russia" rather than a reflection on a redwing or a grackle by the Connecticut River. In this context, it may also be worth noting that Noah Webster, to whose major work any reader of Wallace Stevens has been much beholden, was a Hartfordian. The "green belts" and parks of Frederick Law Olmsted and his son provided Stevens with some of the views and vistas that gave him "a sense of the freshness or vividness of life," which he regarded as a "pure" and "valid purpose for poetry." With a host of Hartford Beechers, however, and the formidable Lydia Huntley Sigourney, Stevens could have had little in common, including his particular sense of the place itself.

Stevens liked Hartford, although he occasionally complained that "one shrivels up living in the same spot, following the same routine"; and as early as 1921 he defined "The malady of the quotidian" in "The Man Whose Pharynx Was Bad":

> The time of year has grown indifferent.
> Mildew of summer and the deepening snow
> Are both alike in the routine I know.
> I am too dumbly in my being pent.
>
> The wind attendant on the solstices
> Blows on the shutters of the metropoles,
> Stirring no poet in his sleep, and tolls
> The grand ideas of the villages.[3]

On the other hand, being "so blessedly busy at the office," especially in the last years, kept him from "noticing the absence of a good many precious things"; in a letter dictated at the office, he told Barbara Church:

> It has been raining ever since you sailed, and right now it is
> ready to start all over again, after an early morning thunder-
> shower. How fortunate I am, in such weather, to have the
> office where one lives in a sort of vacuum, containing nothing
> but the pastime of work. The great building is like a neutral
> zone, invulnerable to the weather. The leaves outdoors seen
> through the windows, belong to a perishable landscape, come
> from nowhere. My pen and inkwell and my blotter and
> memorandum pads are what count. Every now and then, a
> colored boy places fresh mail on my desk, like a planet
> passing at night and casting its light on objects, but with
> more meanings than any planet.
>
> (L, p. 776)

On the way to and from the office, and in the garden, he was attentive to changes, with their "effortless weather," upon which making notes toward a supreme fiction often seemed to depend. Not that the poems were about the weather as such; but the weather was in them. Frequently they served to "demonstrate that just as objects in nature affect us, ... so ... we affect objects in nature, by projecting our moods, emotions, etc. . . .," which he told Harriet Monroe was "the point" of "Three Travelers Watch a Sunrise." Nearly twenty years later, in 1935, he said:

> It is an old story that we derive our ideas of nobility, say, from noble objects of nature. But then, it is an equally old story that we derive them from ourselves. For convenience, and in view of the simplicity of the large mass of people, we give our good qualities to God, or to various gods, but they come from ourselves.
>
> (L, p. 295)

Such a view "propose[d] for study the poet's sense of the world as the source of poetry" in theory as well as in practice—for practice, as the example of any poet of stature will show, precedes the formulation of theory, although Stevens had long been aware that "If I could create an actuality, it would be quite a different world in a good many ways from the world about us." He had characterized Crispin, the hero of "The Comedian as the Letter C," as "a profitless philosopher" because "Life was not for him a straight course; it was picking his way in a haphazard manner through a mass of irrelevancies. Under such circumstances, life would mean nothing to him, however pleasant it might be." In contrast, "In 'The Idea of Order at Key West' life [had] ceased to be a matter of chance," by which Stevens meant that he had "introduce[d] his own order into the life about him," like everyone else, "and that the idea of order in general [was] simply what Bishop Berkeley might have called a fortuitous concourse of personal orders," but not "part of a general order." He also thought that even the perceptive critics of *Ideas of Order* did not "see the kind of world in which [he was] living" in 1935. Nevertheless, if life never became for him quite the "straight course" he wanted it to be—as he admitted in the introduction to *The Necessary Angel*—the "excited ambitions" he entertained for "the theory of poetry, as a subject for study," and for "poetry itself, the naked poem, the imagination manifesting itself in its domination of words," could be cultivated in Hartford.

That he cherished his privacy hardly requires justification. That he seemed to some of the local literati uncommunicative to the point of rudeness is true. Still, when I came to Trinity and put off writing to him, he took the trouble to write to me. "When I noticed in the newspaper last fall," he said, "that you were coming to Hartford I thought that I should see something of you but I suppose that it is like living in Boston without ever getting to see Bunker Hill." It had been easy to sense from earlier correspondence and an hour in the garden at Westerly Terrace that he preferred "to be interested in things of his own choice"; and his letter, as it proved, made it easier to see him thereafter.

It sometimes seems that he found it hard to overcome his natural reserve and diffidence except in letters; but he was not one "to feign an aura of mystery just to build a legend about his name." He admitted to a dislike of "back-slapping"; in an interview given for publication he took a view of his refusal to help celebrate Robert Frost's eightieth birthday quite different from the one already cited. He said:

> I didn't accept because the invitation said the banquet was being held for Mr. Frost's "old friends." I like Mr. Frost, as everyone else does, but by no stretch of the imagination could I call myself one of his old friends. If I had gone, his real "old friends" would have recognized that and resented my pose.[4]

In the later years, it was probably Henry Church whose friendship he cherished most. Church was, Stevens said, the man who had "so thoroughly lived the life [he himself] would have been glad to live" and was "so much more intricate a personality than any half dozen people . . . [he could] think of put together" that he feared to lose his friendship. Even so, it was almost impossible for him to ask the Churches to visit him and Mrs. Stevens in Hartford; and the one occasion on which they did come seems to have been almost a disaster. "I am not really a tyrant," Stevens later told Church, "after all, it took me till after one o'clock the night you were with us to get things straightened out, so that I still think such things are impossible" (L, p. 453).

He had a genuine dislike of the "cheap publicity" and "dreadfully public glare" of "the literary life," even before he became a legend. When he was "beginning again" as a poet in the 1930s, he confessed to feeling that he was "A most inappropriate man / In a most unpropitious place," as he put it in "Sailing after Lunch," partly because he felt out of touch and out of sympathy with the prevailing artistic climate. His "nerves" did not "shrink from loud sounds" or "strong colors," nor did he prefer "a drizzle in Venice to a hard rain in Hartford"; but "aesthetic self-consciousness," whether of the left or right or of the kind manifested by some of the people who attended the premiere of *Four Saints in Three Acts*, was unpalatable. He vented his spleen on the latter in a letter to Harriet Monroe:

> There were . . . numerous asses of the first water in the audience. New York sent a trainload of people of this sort to

Hartford; people who walked round with cigarette holders a foot long, and so on. After all, if there is any place under the sun that needs debunking, it is the place where people of this sort come to and go to.

(L, p. 267)

II

Stevens was acutely aware not only of the "asses" and of salesmen in New York galleries "disguised as catalogues or as chairs," but also of "people who live only in the corporeal world, enjoying the wind and the weather and supplying standards of normality"; that is, the "they" who insist to the man with the blue guitar:

> "play, you must,
> A tune beyond us, yet ourselves,
>
> A tune upon the blue guitar
> Of things exactly as they are."

(CP, p. 165)

Such a "they" would also include the people in a photograph, recalled in a letter to Hi Simons, of "a lot of fat men and women in the woods, drinking beer and singing Hi-li Hi-lo," which "convince[d him] that there [was] a normal that [he] ought to try to achieve," however much opposed he was to "think[ing] that we should insist that the poet is normal or, for that matter, that anybody is."

He always possessed a strong sense of his own identity. Even at the age of twenty, when he had just arrived in New York from Harvard and was wondering whether "literature [was] really a profession" and whether "you single it out, or must . . . let it decide in you for itself," he was "determined . . . not to *try* to suit anybody except [himself]." Nearly fifty years later, in his Bergen lecture at Yale, he was still concerned with the consequences of that choice, when he said:

> A man's sense of the world is born with him and persists, and penetrates the ameliorations of education and experience of life. His species is as fixed as his genus. For each man, then, certain subjects are congenital. Now, the poet manifests his personality, first of all, by his choice of subject. Temperament is a more explicit word than personality and would no doubt be the exact word to use, since it emphasizes the manner of thinking and feeling. It is agreeable to think of

· 10 ·

the poet as a whole biological mechanism and not as a
subordinate mechanism within that larger one.
Temperament, too, has attracted a pejorative meaning.[5]

His sense of the world was broad enough, to begin with, to accommodate views sometimes held to be mutually exclusive. If one makes
allowances for the youthful tone and manner, a passage from his journal
for 1900 suggests that breadth fairly accurately:

> Sometimes I wish I wore no crown—that I trod on
> something thicker than air—that there were no robins, or
> peach dumplings, or violets in my world—that I was the
> proprietor of a patent medicine store—or manufactured
> pants for the trade—and that my name was Asa Snuff. But
> alas! the tormenting harmonies sweep around my hat, my
> bosom swells with "agonies and exultations"— and I pose.
>
> (L, p. 48)

"Most people," however, remained "a great nuisance" and, he added,
"my own disposition is not remarkably lenient in such things. Perhaps
that is why my own likes are more often for things than for people:
because of intolerance." At twenty-seven, he had discovered that "Old
people are tremendous frauds" and that "The point is to be young—and
to be a little in love, or very much—and to desire carnations and
'creations'—and to be glad when spring comes." His "idea of life" could
include, in addition to "a fine evening, an orchestra . . . [and] a medium
dinner," "a crowd *at a distance*," although in his bleakest mood,
"people" reduced him to indignation:

> One sees the most painful people, wherever one goes.
> Human qualities, on an average, are fearful subjects for
> contemplation. Deceit—how inevitable! Pride, lack of so-
> phistication, ignorance, egoism—What dreadful things!
> Necessity, too.
>
> (L, p. 86)

It is not surprising, then, that poetry came to be "a form of retreat"
and provided an opportunity to "let go" in which "the judgment of other
people [was] neither here nor there," at least during the years in which
he was writing for "the grand poem" the "preliminary minutiae" that
became *Harmonium*, published less than a month before his forty-
fourth birthday. His decision to stop writing, despite the failure of

Harmonium, and his determination to get ahead in business still give his critics pause. He himself said, "when I really was a poet in the sense that I was all imagination, and so on, I deliberately gave up writing poetry because, much as I loved it, there were too many other things I wanted not to make an effort to have them." Florida continued to be a place to enjoy "mere being," even after he had begun to write again, at least until he made his formal "Farewell" in the poem he placed at the beginning of the 1936 edition of *Ideas of Order*. But Hartford and his "leafless North," its "wintry slime / Both of men and clouds, a slime of men in crowds," and "the violent mind / That is their mind," proved more difficult to "imagine well" than he expected.

It was, again, his Bergen lecture that suggested the nature of his solution by an analogy he drew between what he called "our world" and "the poet's world":

> We could not speak of our world as something to be
> distinguished from the poet's sense of it unless we justified it
> and recognized it as having an existence apart from the
> projection of his personality, as land and sea, sky and cloud.
> He himself desires to make the distinction as part of the
> process of realizing himself. Once the distinction has been
> made, it becomes an instrument for the exploration of poetry.
> By means of it we can determine the relation of the poet to his
> subject. This would be simple if he wrote about his own
> world. We would compare it with ours. But what he writes
> about is his sense of our world.
>
> (NA, pp. 118–19)

Relation by analogy, it is obvious, had its privileges as well as its perils and problems. The asperity with which he frequently viewed "our world" sometimes came close to misanthropy, as in "The Mechanical Optimist":

> A lady dying of diabetes
> Listened to the radio,
> Catching the lesser dithyrambs.
> So heaven collects its bleating lambs.
>
> Her useless bracelets fondly fluttered,
> Paddling the melodic swirls,
> The idea of god no longer sputtered
> At the roots of her indifferent curls.
>
> (CP, p. 184)

The hapless vulgarity of this figure, incidentally, seemed to imitate somewhat unbecomingly T. S. Eliot's style in portraiture. In "Mystic Garden & Middling Beast," he looked at an "unedifying" Hartford with an equally disaffected glance!

> The poet striding among the cigar stores,
> Ryan's lunch, hatters, insurance, and medicines,
> Denies that abstraction is a vice except
> To the fatuous. . . .
>   (CP, p. 185)

He devoted a whole volume to working out and clarifying the poet's sense of our world as a subject. *Parts of a World* has seemed to many readers a miscellany of "theoretical exercises" leading up to *Notes toward a Supreme Fiction*. On the other hand, it provides texts of unusual interest and pertinence in defining Stevens' sense of "our world," not only Hartford and Connecticut but also "our climate," and foreshadows the way "A mythology reflects its region," as he put it in one of his last poems.

Ideas of Order had provided intimations of the local scene, including some notes on municipal sculpture and public monuments by a former

> hunter of those sovereigns of the soul
> And savings banks, Fides, the sculptor's prize,
> All eyes and size, and galled Justitia,
> Trained to poise the tables of the law,
> Patientia, forever soothing wounds,
> And mighty Fortitudo, frantic bass . . .
>   (CP, p. 124)

as well as one company's guardian lions, if not the Hartford's caribou. It also includes a good deal of autumn and winter weather: "The skreak and skritter of evening gone / And grackles gone . . . ," "wind and frost . . . in mornings of angular ice / That passed beyond us through the narrow sky," and "the east wind blowing round one"; and some of those indeterminate days in New England, when

> The sun is seeking something bright to shine on.
> The trees are wooden, the grass is yellow and thin.
> The ponds are not the surfaces it seeks.
> It must create its colors out of itself.
>   (CP, pp. 157–58)

In *Parts of a World* the observing eye was as often the eye of the painter as it was the eye of the walker. In "Of Hartford in a Purple Light,"

> A moment ago, light masculine,
> Working, with big hands, on the town,
> Arranged its heroic attitudes.
>
> But now as in an amour of women
> Purple sets purple round. Look, Master,
> See the river, the railroad, the cathedral . . .
> . . . .
> Hi! Whisk it, poodle, flick the spray
> Of the ocean, ever-freshening,
> On the irised hunks, the stone bouquet.
>> (CP, p. 227)

Such an early morning view tempts one to propose this "illustration of the poetic as a sense" as Stevens' equivalent of "Composed upon Westminster Bridge," although "Master Soleil" as poodle suggests something more nearly akin to Dufy. "The Common Life," another such "illustration," caught the downtown skyline (as it used to be in the thirties) from a perspective that recalls the drawings of Paul Klee:

> That's the down-town frieze,
> Principally the church steeple,
> A black line beside a white line;
> And the stack of the electric plant,
> A black line drawn on flat air.
>> (CP, p. 221)

In the first stanza of "The Poems of Our Climate," the light that creates the unity of the scene is, without having to be overtly so designated, familiar to any New Englander:

> Clear water in a brilliant bowl,
> Pink and white carnations. The light
> In the room more like a snowy air,
> Reflecting snow. A newly-fallen snow
> At the end of winter when afternoons return [,]
>> (CP, p. 193)

· 14 ·

when "one desires / So much more" than "A world of clear water, brilliant-edged / . . . more than a world of white and snowy scents." For "The never-resting mind," "to be young . . . and to desire carnations and 'creations' " was no longer "the point," as it had been thirty years before; and

> in this bitterness, delight
> Since the imperfect is so hot in us,
> Lies in flawed words and stubborn sounds.
>
> (CP, p. 194)

In "Connoisseur of Chaos," "the flowers of South Africa" are "bright / On the tables of Connecticut" and "it all" goes on "in an orderly way." In "Anything is Beautiful If You Say It Is," it is "I," the eye:

> I love the metal grapes,
> The rusty battered shapes
> Of the pears and of the cheese
>
> And the window's lemon light,
> The very will of the nerves,
> The crack across the pane,
> The dirt along the sill.
>
> (CP, p. 211)

And in "The Glass of Water," the poet, addressed as "fat Jocundus, worrying / About what stands here . . . / . . . in the centre of our lives, this time, this day," is reminded that

> It is a state, this spring among the politicians
> Playing cards. In a village of the indigenes,
> One would have still to discover. Among the dogs and dung,
> One would continue to contend with one's ideas.
>
> (CP, p. 198)

Being a poet had been easier when Stevens had been "all imagination and so on" and "in a most excellent state of spontaneity," as he had said of the effect of "long summer spells of quiet" when he sent Knopf the manuscript of *Harmonium*. Now the momentum of his mind seemed to be "all toward abstraction." What saved him from mere abstraction was the renewed confirmation in himself of a quality he valued in William Carlos Williams, whom he had also—to Williams' displeasure—

characterized as "anti-poetic" and "sentimental" as well as "romantic." The romantic poet in 1934, Stevens said,

> happens to be one who still dwells in an ivory tower, but who insists that life would be intolerable except for the fact that one has, from the top, such an exceptional view of the public dump and the advertising signs of Snider's Catsup, Ivory Snow and Chevrolet Cars; he is the hermit who dwells alone with the sun and moon, but insists on taking a rotten newspaper.[6]

Taken together, the poems of *Parts of a World* provided an opportunity to work out in increasingly complex ways both "the opposition between things as they are and things imagined" and the "incessant conjunctions between" them as well as a means of discovering a perspective from which one could feel, like "the man on the dump," the "purifying change" between one's disgust for "the things / That are on the dump (azaleas and so on) / And those that will be (azaleas and so on)" when "One rejects / The trash." He said in a variation on "The Man on the Dump" which he titled "The Latest Freed Man":

> It was how he was free. It was how his freedom came.
> It was being without description, being an ox.
> It was the importance of the trees outdoors,
> The freshness of the oak-leaves, not so much
> That they were oak-leaves, as the way they looked.
> It was everything being more real, himself
> At the centre of reality, seeing it.
> It was everything bulging and blazing and big in itself,
> The blue of the rug, the portrait of Vidal,
> *Qui fait fi des joliesses banales*, the chairs.
> (CP, p. 205)

It would become, indeed, "everything" seen first with "an ignorant eye," then with "a will to change," so that

> The freshness of transformation is
>
> The freshness of a world. It is our own,
> It is ourselves, the freshness of ourselves,
> (CP, pp. 397–98)

and what we see—"a kind / Of volatile world, too constant to be denied"—"Are rubbings of a glass in which we peer," till finally

> . . . the going round
>
> And round and round, the merely going round,
> Until merely going round is a final good,
> The way wine comes at a table in a wood.
>
> And we enjoy like men, the way a leaf
> Above the table spins its constant spin,
> So that we look at it with pleasure, look
>
> At it spinning its eccentric measure.
> (CP, pp. 405–06)

And we hear the poet's name for his supreme fiction, "my green, my fluent mundo."

III

The poems that make up *Parts of a World* occupied Stevens for about five years; it took him just four months to complete *Notes toward a Supreme Fiction*. He had not only recovered his poetic balance; he had become—outside of Hartford still, and for the most part in the milieu of the literary journals—a poet to be reckoned with. His reluctance to discuss his work on the ground that "explanations spoil things" gave way before the serious inquiries of Hi Simons, who had begun the first full-length study of the poetry. His friendship with Henry Church began in 1939, when Church asked permission to print translations of poems from *Harmonium* for an American number of *Mesures*. Old friends with whom he had jaunted in Florida were in touch; and with some of them he found it easy to "let go," as he did to one who sent him persimmons from Georgia:

> Wild persimmons make one feel like a hungry man in the woods. As I ate them, I thought of opossums and birds, and the antique Japanese prints in black and white, in which monkeys are eating persimmons in bare trees. There is nothing more desolate than a persimmon tree, with the old

ripe fruit hanging on it. As you see, there is such a thing as
being a spiritual epicure.

(L, p. 394)

The landscapes of *Notes toward a Supreme Fiction* ranged from
Hartford to a Ceylon imagined from postcards, books, and letters sent by
his friend Leonard van Geyzel of Lunawila and to "a blue island in a
sky-wide water" in a remembered South. Much of the weather was "by
Franz Hals, / Brushed up by brushy winds in brushy clouds, / Wetted by
blue, colder for white," when "Gay is, gay was, the gay forsythia / And
yellow, yellow thins the northern blue." For the poet, "A bench"—
presumably in Elizabeth Park—"was his catalepsy, Theatre / Of
Trope," and

> The water of
> The lake was full of artificial things,
>
> Like a page of music, like an upper air,
> Like a momentary color, in which swans
> Were seraphs, were saints, were changing essences.

(CP, p. 397)

In the poems that followed *Notes*, "the poet's world" continued to
expand. For the first time, really, something like nostalgia for a world
"in which the characters speak because they want / To speak . . . Free
for a moment, from malice and sudden cry, / Complete in a completed
scene, speaking / Their parts as in a youthful happiness" began to make
itself felt. It was a world in which, as unexpected "favors" dropped from
his growing interest in genealogy and family history, recollections of
the world he had long ago "lost" when he left Reading began to alter the
tone and therefore the substance of his work.

As a lonely young lawyer in New York still somewhat uncertain of his
future, he had "Every Spring . . . a month or two of semi-blackness," and
he found it easy to recall how "Some of us used to lie in the sun at
Kissinger's Locks a whole summer long, going home only for meals and
to sleep" and to "feel the warmth . . . and remember the laziness of it."
He told his fiancée:

> The Low-Germans . . . are very common at home. True-
> heartedness surely describes them. I love them, my dear.

. . . I feel my kinship, my race. To study them is to realize one's own identity.

(L, p. 127)

Reading was very much on his mind during the months before his marriage, partly because he knew that Elsie was reluctant to think of losing touch with *her* world and because he wanted to prepare her for the great change that life in the city would involve; but it also gave him genuine pleasure to recall the world *he* had lost. He knew that Reading offered him no prospects of living the kind of life he wanted to live; and it seems likely that Elsie came to understand this, for among the passages she copied from his early letters before destroying them was one that simply confirmed his ambition—"I should like to make a music of my own, a literature of my own, and I should like to live my own life"—an ambition he continued to cherish almost to the end of his life.

The whole of which Reading was a part, like his grandfather's farm "and the people who lived in it," which he told Thornton Wilder he "look[ed] back to . . . the way American literature used to look back to English literature," remained buried for a long time. Except for a fleeting reminiscence of local idiom, almost the only allusion to that world came in the setting of "Three Travelers Watch a Sunrise" that "represent[ed] a forest of heavy trees on a hilltop in eastern Pennsylvania" and that seemed to some critics an odd backdrop for a discussion of poetry at four o'clock in the morning by three Chinese in "costumes of silk, red, blue, and green" who illustrated the significant points of their discourse with a melon and a red porcelain water bottle. That bit of perversity would seem to have been suggested partly by the Chinese pagoda at the summit of Mount Penn. Thirty years later, in "A Completely New Set of Objects," he recalled the annual festivals on the Schuylkill River, "down which paraded canoes and boats lighted at night with candled Chinese lanterns":

> From a Schuylkill in mid-earth there came emerging
> Flotillas, willed and wanted, bearing in them
>
> Shadows of friends, of those he knew, each bringing
> From the water in which he believed and out of desire
>
> Things made by mid-terrestrial, mid-human
> Makers without knowing, or intending, uses.

> These figures verdant with time's buried verdure
> Came paddling their canoes, a thousand thousand,
>
> Carrying such shapes, of such alleviation,
> That the beholder knew their subtle purpose,
>
> Knew well the shapes were the exactest shaping
> Of a vast people old in meditation . . .
>
> Under Tinicum or small Cohansey,
> The fathers of the makers may lie and weather.
>
> (CP, pp. 352–53)

Such re-creations of the past came both opportunely and naturally, at a moment when, as he put it in "Debris of Life and Mind,"

> There is so little that is close and warm.
> It is as if we were never children.
>
> Sit in the room. It is true in the moonlight
> That it is as if we had never been young.
> We ought not to be awake.
>
> . . . .
> Stay here. Speak of familiar things a while.
>
> (CP, p. 338)

How much the sudden access of the past contributed to the "closeness" and "warmth" and "familiarity" of the later and last poems may be difficult to judge; but that it played a large part in deepening Stevens' tone to one "that confesses openly all the bitter secretions of experience" and seems to be "a present perfecting, a satisfaction in the irremediable poverty of life" is not to be denied. "Credences of Summer," "The Auroras of Autumn," "To an Old Philosopher in Rome," "The Rock," and, I think, in its autumnally austere way, "An Ordinary Evening in New Haven" are works in which the poet's feeling toward his subject seems to have been so intense that "one is willing for [them] to be what [they are]" without cavil as to their "significance" or "importance." What is true of these longer poems is equally true of many of the shorter poems; they are "secretions of insight" that momentarily "compose the world," in which "the poet" becomes "the intermediary between people and the world in which they live and also between people as between themselves; but not," as Stevens added, "between people and some other world."

The end of the war restored some connections and brought some unlooked-for changes. Although his old bookseller, M. Vidal, had died in the fall of 1944, Vidal's daughter carried on the business and kept Stevens in touch with his "imagined" and "imaginary" Paris, choosing paintings for his collection and sending him whatever books he wanted. The death of Hi Simons in the spring of 1945, however, troubled him. The death of Henry Church in the spring of 1947 was a much keener loss; but he continued to correspond with Mrs. Church to the end of his life, with great pleasure. His correspondence, indeed, increased; and he continued to write poems. He told José Rodríguez Feo that he "really read very much less of everything than most people. It is more interesting," he concluded, "to sit round and look out of the window." In a letter to Mrs. Church a few months after her husband's death, he said:

> You must not allow yourself to become one more solitary
> person [at Ville d'Avray, the Churches' home in France and,
> for Stevens, as he added, "wholly a fiction, but, because of
> Corot . . . a very special fiction"]. The ordinary interest in a
> solitary life becomes accentuated in a place full of agreeable
> communications—I don't mean memories, but the insights
> and feelings that we have in the midst of difficulties in a spot
> that happens to be just the right spot for us. The true
> happiness to be found in such a spot is the sense that it
> restores and strengthens.
>
> (L, p. 563)

Hartford was, for the most part, "the right spot" for Stevens. The communications he received there, especially those that pleased him, even provided him with ways of dealing with unforeseen and occasionally unwelcome requests, such as an invitation to contribute to the Ezra Pound issue of the *Quarterly Review of Literature*. In his refusal he said:

> A friend has just written to me from France speaking of
>   "My pink Persian cat . . . in front of me, looking up
> just now with his reproachful amber eyes. He does not like to
> be molested even by thoughts or looks."
>   That's Pound.
>
> (L, p. 565)

On the other hand, much that was going on in painting and poetry seemed to him "very queer" and "lurid and rhetorical," "just so much frustration and evasion"; and, he added, that applied "even to politics." He needed, in the most literal sense of the word, a change, although he could make something even of his feeling of "aridity" and "monotony." He feared the "total freedom" of the postwar world because "the great critical and expository minds that our time so greatly needs do not seem to exist." So long, then, as he could "compose" his feelings, he could cope. He wrote to Rodríguez Feo in the fall of 1948:

> At the moment I feel completely illiterate, so to speak. I rather think that nature gets at me more thoroughly now than at any other time of the year. One grows used to spring; and summer and winter become bores. But Otonno! How this oozing away hurts notwithstanding the pumpkins and the glaciale of frost and the onslaught of books and pictures and music and people. It is finished, Zarathustra says; and one goes to the Canoe Club and has a couple of Martinis and a pork chop and looks down the spaces of the river and participates in the disintegration, the decomposition, the rapt finale. Murder . . . and adieu; assassination . . . and farewell.
>
> (L, p. 621)

At the Canoe Club, he used to tell his guests, particularly those who belonged to the academy, one did not talk about poetry; one appreciated the photographs and pinups behind the bar. No one, of course, violated that prohibition more readily than Stevens himself; and in the last years he enjoyed the comments on his work by fellow vice-presidents and presidents who had not only read it but could talk sensibly about it.

It is true that the "essential poem at the centre of things," which he postulated and projected with such expectancy in "A Primitive like an Orb," continued to elude him; but it remained a symbol of his self—or, as he said, "of one of [his] selves." "What We See Is What We Think" was not simply the title of a poem; it was an axiom. His description of an ideal reader of a fiction applied to the kind of maker he admired even more precisely: He was one

> for whom the story and the other meaning should come together like two aspects that combine to produce a third or, if they do not combine, inter-act, so that one influences the other and produces an effect similar in kind to the prismatic

formations that occur about us in nature in the case of
reflections and refractions.

(NA, p. 109)

A poem written with these "prismatic formations" in mind could also
be characterized as "the poem of the idea within the poem of words," as
an illustration of the proposition that "the world is what you make of it"
or a demonstration of "the imagination pressing back against the
pressure of reality."

If, in a sense, at least from 1930 on, his poetry had been based most
often on what he called "theory" and "propositions about life," he could
as an old poet "sit in a park and listen to the locusts; . . . sit in a park and
hear church bells" and wonder whether this would be "two pasts or one
present and one past." He could go to Elizabeth Park, which "is almost
all there is in Hartford" and which he liked "especially on Sundays
when people go there," and see that "The very fat woman who exercises
her dog had a new dress on yesterday. The tennis courts were full. A
little boy ran after squirrels and called them: Cats." He could "pretend
that everything in nature is artificial and that everything artifical is
natural, as, for example, that the roses in Elizabeth Park are placed there
daily by some lover of mankind and that Paris is an eruption of nature."
He could watch some nuns painting water lilies or could consider "The
Plain Sense of Things":

> After the leaves have fallen, we return
> To a plain sense of things. It is as if
> We had come to an end of the imagination,
> Inanimate in an inert savoir.
>
> It is difficult even to choose the adjective
> For this blank cold, this sadness without cause.
> The great structure has become a minor house.
> No turban walks across the lessened floors.
>
> The greenhouse never so badly needed paint.
> The chimney is fifty years old and slants to one side.
> A fantastic effort has failed, a repetition
> In a repetitiousness of men and flies.
>
> Yet the absence of the imagination had
> Itself to be imagined. The great pond,
> The plain sense of it, without reflections, leaves,

Mud, water like dirty glass, expressing silence

Of a sort, silence of a rat come out to see,
The great pond and its waste of the lilies, all this
Had to be imagined as an inevitable knowledge,
Required, as a necessity requires.

(CP, pp. 502-03)

It would not be "every day" that "the world arrange[d] itself in a poem." And it did not matter that his work remained "indefinite," that it had "not got anywhere" philosophically. "What we all need," he said in the spring of 1955, "is to find that in which we can be easily fecund."

He had in fact come to terms with himself, with his own life, and, therefore, from his perspective, with the world. Having accomplished that reconciliation, he found it possible and pleasant, in Hartford, Connecticut, to "feel like a native," as he said in the piece written for the Voice of America in the spring of 1955. It was easy, too, to be himself; he could appreciate not only the place but the spirit of the place, the sense that "we live in the tradition which is the true mythology of the region and we breathe in with every breath the joy of having ourselves been created by what has been endured and mastered in the past." He had made "The transition from make believe for one's self to make believe for others," which was, with a qualification altogether characteristic, "the beginning, or the end, of poetry in the individual."

It is hard to choose, now, a way of concluding. His sense of the place was more than the sum of its parts. There is, however, "A Clear Day and No Memories," in which we—for he includes us, too—can share his solitude and in which, as so often in the last poems by the merest allusion, the life he had lived in the mind and most unforgettably in the imagination is momentarily evoked, as in the very mention of what is not thought. Here it may be the beloved in her "blue-shadowed silk" for whom Peter Quince improvised so many years before at the clavier:

No soldiers in the scenery,
No thoughts of people now dead,
As they were fifty years ago,
Young and living in a live air,
Young and walking in the sunshine,
Bending in blue dresses to touch something,
Today the mind is not part of the weather.

Today the air is clear of everything.
It has no knowledge except of nothingness
And it flows over us without meanings,
As if none of us had ever been here before
And are not now: in this shallow spectacle,
This invisible activity, this sense.

(OP, p. 113)

NOTES

1. Wallace Stevens, *Letters of Wallace Stevens*, ed. Holly Stevens (New York: Knopf, 1966), p. 835; hereafter cited as L.
2. Cited in *On Common Ground: A Selection of Hartford Writers*, ed. Alice DeLana and Cynthia Reik (Hartford: The Stowe-Day Foundation, 1975), p. 125.
3. Wallace Stevens, *The Collected Poems of Wallace Stevens* (New York: Knopf, 1954), p. 96; hereafter cited as CP.
4. *The Trinity Review: A Celebration for Wallace Stevens*, 8 (May 1954), 29.
5. Wallace Stevens, "Effects of Analogy," in *The Necessary Angel* (New York: Knopf, 1951), p. 120; hereafter cited as NA.
6. Wallace Stevens, "Williams," in *Opus Posthumous*, ed. Samuel French Morse (New York: Knopf, 1957), p. 256; hereafter cited as OP.

FRANK DOGGETT AND DOROTHY EMERSON

About Stevens' Comments on Several Poems

I

Stevens' remarks about his poems have an air of latent disclosure. Even when most significant, they are oblique, laconic, and offer limitations more often than information. Most of his comments are about poems in the first four books and *Notes toward a Supreme Fiction*. He has very little to say about the poems in his last two books. All his comments have the intrinsic value of emanating from his own private understanding of what he created. No matter how reticent they may be, they tell or hint much about his poems that otherwise might be overlooked. Both comment and poem require analysis and reflect meaning on each other and, at times, on other poems.

A statement about "How to Live. What to Do," for instance, has the privity that can only be the poet's. Stevens explained to Ronald Lane Latimer that he preferred this poem to the others in *Ideas of Order*. "I like it most, I suppose, because it so definitely represents my way of thinking."[1] "Way of thinking" has two meanings: a kind of thinking and also a method of presenting that thinking. What is especially revealing about Stevens' remark is that it shows his consciousness of his own characteristics: of the way he proceeded in thought and the devices, the little scenes that present his thought.

What is the "way of thinking" in the first sense that is so typical of Stevens? Several critics have described Stevens' tendency to proceed in the discourse of his poems by reduction.[2] Certainly a number of Stevens' early deliberations in poetry move toward a diminution of various kinds. There is an abatement in "Sunday Morning" from "The need of some imperishable bliss" to a sense of our "old dependency of day and night." "The Comedian as the Letter C" deflates the status of humanity from "man is the intelligence of his soil" to "his soil is man's intelligence." For the poet of "Le Monocle de Mon Oncle," the "measure of the intensity of love / Is measure, also, of the verve of earth." But that intensity has subsided and he can say, "For me, the firefly's quick, electric stroke / Ticks tediously the time of one more year."

Stevens' reductive poems at times have a flow of thought through disillusion and the stinting of any grandiloquence until a minimum or a poverty of being is asserted as value. "Not to have is the beginning of desire," he asserts in *Notes toward a Supreme Fiction*. Later in "An Ordinary Evening in New Haven" he sees desire as a state that provokes imaginative acts: "The points of vision and desire are the same." Because reduction leads to the kind of destitution that induces creativity, the poet in him seems to be saying "Bare night is best. Bare earth is best. Bare, bare" for then "the voice that is great within us rises up."[3]

Rejection is one of Stevens' modes of achieving the desired reduction. In "How to Live. What to Do" there is an implied repudiation of the moon in the word "impure." The impure moon is a symbol of the imagination whose light casts illusion on reality.

> Last evening the moon rose above this rock
> Impure upon a world unpurged.
> The man and his companion stopped
> To rest before the heroic height.
>
> (CP, p. 125)

The height is heroic, like the sound of the wind in the last stanza, because it is reality apart from any conception of it, and hence it is exalted above human error in the land below. The two persons in the poem are identified only in their rejection of the "flame-freaked sun"—a distorted conception of reality—and their ascent above "the muck of the land"—a pejorative and descriptive phrase. Priest, crested image, and voices are left behind as the two ascend above fiction and misconception. They hope to find a "sun of fuller fire," a comprehension of reality unblemished by human adhesions. Instead there is a reduction to essence and image, for at the peak there is only the rock and the wind.

> There was neither voice nor crested image,
> No chorister, nor priest. There was
> Only the great height of the rock
> And the two of them standing still to rest.
>
> (CP, p. 126)

In the poem's conclusion, the cold wind is an early version of the cold, invincible wind of "The Auroras of Autumn." It is joyous because that is the sense of the natural world for Stevens.

> There was the cold wind and the sound
> It made, away from the muck of the land
> That they had left, heroic sound
> Joyous and jubilant and sure.
>
> (CP, p. 126)

"How to Live. What to Do" presents its reductive flow of discourse through a metaphor that compares the rejections of old illusions to an ascent to a summit. This kind of presentation—a metaphorical scene or anecdote—is the other aspect of the ambiguity in Stevens' statement that "How to Live. What to Do" represented so definitely his "way of thinking." Sixteen years later, he described the presentation of idea that he thought was appropriate for a poet. "A poet's natural way of thinking is by way of figures, and while this includes figures of speech it also includes examples, illustrations and parallel cases generally."[4] "Illustrations and parallel cases" are important to any study of his poetry, but they are especially useful in understanding his remarks about "How to Live. What to Do" and "Some Friends from Pascagoula."

Stevens usually illustrates his meditations in poetry by an action or a scene that is a metaphor for its idea. Another metaphor of ascent that presents the idea of reduction is found in "Extracts from Addresses to the Academy of Fine Ideas." Here the poet considers that "if one went to the moon, / Or anywhere beyond," all remnants of old thought and its delusions—all ideas, in fact—would be lost in the alien environment, and thus one would be empty of all concepts, all beliefs. "One would be drowned in the air of difference" (CP, p. 258). Then if one returned, free of any memory of conceptions or even of perceptions, all delusions vanished, with complete reduction to the minimum of being, life itself refreshed as in its first idea would return from the first breath that inhaled the tenuous essence of reality.

> And naked of any illusion, in poverty,
> In the exactest poverty, if then
> One breathed the cold evening, the deepest inhalation
> Would come from that return to the subtle centre.
>
> (CP, p. 258)

II

The metaphor of ascent as an illustration of reductive thinking appears in another poem in *Parts of a World*, "Mrs. Alfred Uraguy": "The moonlight crumpled to degenerate forms / While she approached the real upon her mountain" (CP, p. 249). In counterbalance this poem also contains a descent into the imagination and its fecundity by a youth "Rushing from what was real" down to "The ultimate elegance: the imagined land."

Descent as a metaphor associated with the idea of augmentation had already been depicted by Stevens in a poem in *Ideas of Order*. This poem, "Some Friends from Pascagoula," follows immediately after "How to Live. What to Do." "The arrangement is simply based on contrast," Stevens says of his placement of poems in *Ideas of Order* (L, p. 279). Contrary to the use of an ascending figure to illustrate a movement toward reduction, the descent of this poem is a trope representative of an idea of aggrandizement of an ordinary event, the descent of an eagle, given as an image of nobility by virtue of its imaginative presentation in the language of poetry.

Stevens' comment on "Some Friends from Pascagoula," like his comment on "How to Live. What to Do," has an air of offering a private revelation. Ultimately, the disclosure is withheld because the comment offers mostly negative information. The poet tells what he did not intend; and what he does tell about the poem is divulged in terminology that seems to have a special meaning. This restricted information must be interpreted reciprocally with the poem. "Some Friends from Pascagoula" is "neither merely description nor symbolical," he says. The phrase "merely description" suggests that the poet had in mind some other, more intense or informative kind of meaning. "What seems to be mere description is, after all, a presentation of a 'sovereign sight' " (L, p. 349). "Sovereign sight" is a quotation from the poem; the key word is "presentation" and because Stevens opposes it to symbolism or description it apparently indicates to him some kind of method or device for offering a concept. The sense of the word here seems to be the act of setting forth for the mind's attention an event of literary or artistic significance. The "more" of the first line of the poem implies that what has already been reported has some special allure for the one who is speaking the poem.

> Tell me more of the eagle, Cotton,
> And you, black Sly,

Tell me how he descended
Out of the morning sky.
(CP, p. 126)

The speaker of the poem seeks an enhancement of an everyday happening that he exalts by his own request. He asks of Cotton and black Sly that they tell him with the "deepened voice" of poetry and its "noble imagery" more of the descent of the eagle. In the poem, they never answer. The poetry is his alone.

Describe with deepened voice
And noble imagery
His slowly-falling round
Down to the fishy sea.
(CP, p. 126)

The poet's explanation of his poem maintains that it is "an attempt to give a specimen of 'noble imagery' in a commonplace occurrence." Six years after writing the poem, Stevens was still engrossed with the idea of "noble imagery." Several passages of his essay "The Noble Rider and the Sound of Words" can be useful to a reading of the poem; for instance: "We may emerge from our *bassesse* and, if we do, how would it happen if not by the intervention of some fortune of the mind."[5] Perhaps the "fortune of the mind" is enacted by the voice of the speaker of the poem addressing in imaginative language the *bassesse* of Cotton and black Sly. Thus the speaker gives an opulence of the imagination to a "commonplace occurrence," and the descent of the eagle becomes an example of exaltation by means of the language of poetry. It should be remembered that Stevens says, "This is neither merely description nor symbolical." By "this" Stevens may indicate only the eagle and its descent, the poem's anecdote. If so, he could have been afraid that the eagle as the national emblem would insinuate itself into a reading of the poem. If we take Stevens' injunction into account in a broader sense, however, we may assume that the poem offers a "specimen" of a psychological event by a "parallel" case or analogy that is no more than implied. The "parallel" case could be regarded as symbolic meaning and yet not intrude on Stevens' conception of "symbolical" when that conception is considered in the light of his use of the word in other contexts. Stevens denies any symbolic presence in several poems where symbolic meaning is ineluctable, as in the planter poem in "Notes toward a Supreme Fiction." His explanation of the meaning of the statue in "Owl's Clover" indicates a limited symbolic reference more specific than allusive and hence seems to reveal a conception of the function of symbolism akin to allegory or emblem or sign. "In one poem," he says of his use of the statue in "Owl's Clover," "it is a symbol for art; in another for society, etc." (L, p. 355).

If we think of "Some Friends from Pascagoula" as having a possible parallel in a psychological occurrence, then in the analogy the speaker of the poem would become the conscious verbal imagination and the "kinky clan," the creative psyche, would become what Stevens a few months later would identify with subconscious conceptualization: "Night and the imagination being one" (OP, p. 71). In "The News and the Weather," Stevens personifies the subconscious, to use the term he favors, as a black woman, "Solange," who is also a magnolia, "a nigger tree and with a nigger name." Stevens' use of the word "nigger" has no racial significance and is not pejorative. It is his way of referring to the darkness of the unconscious in an amused and colloquial manner.

Stevens says in his comment on "Some Friends from Pascagoula" that "a man without existing conventions (beliefs, etc.) depends for ideas of a new and noble order on 'noble imagery.' " This man could be identified with the verbal imagination and thus with the speaker of the poem, and his dependence on "noble imagery" could be considered a dependence on what is given by his creative imagination personified by Cotton and black Sly. Presentation, in Stevens' use of the word and in this understanding of the poem, offers an image that implies a "parallel" case, with the descent of the eagle supplying the imagery that is exalted in the poem's language. The conscious poetic imagination deriving its ideas of a "noble order" from imagery supplied by the creative unconscious is an intimation that may be derived from that analogy. This device is certainly symbolic in the larger sense of the word; but in Stevens' more restricted sense it is only an analogy from which the intimation springs.

Nine years after writing "Some Friends from Pascagoula" Stevens described devices useful to a poet who might wish to avoid a statement of thought and to speak in a parable that implies concept by analogies. He is referring to Roger Caillois: "he writes poetry that looks like prose. When it comes to thinking a thing out and to stating it simply, he seems invariably to evade direct thinking by lapsing into a metaphor or a parable and, in this way, he proves things, not by expressing reasons but by intimations to be derived from analogies" (L, p. 494). These devices of Caillois' are reminiscent of those Stevens had used in many poems, including "Some Friends from Pascagoula." It is interesting that he does not speak of "intimations to be derived from analogies" as symbolism.

The final stanzas of the poem illustrate what Stevens means by "a sovereign sight" that he says "seems to be mere description":

Say how his heavy wings,
Spread on the sun-bronzed air,
Turned tip and tip away,
Down to the sand, the glare

Of the pine trees edging the sand,
Dropping in sovereign rings
Out of his fiery lair.
Speak of the dazzling wings.

(CP, p. 127)

These stanzas offer the sense of a magnificence appropriate for "noble imagery," and it is the heightened language of poetry that Stevens employs to gain this effect. The "fiery lair" is "noble imagery" for the bright, sunlit sky. The "dazzling wings" signify an enhancement of the eagle in the language of the imagination, an aggrandizement appropriate to the trope of descent in Stevens' use of the trope at that time. This enhancement in language given to an image by the imagination is the "peculiarity" defined as nobility in "The Noble Rider and the Sound of Words": "Yet the imagination gives to everything it touches a peculiarity and it seems to me that the peculiarity of the imagination is nobility, of which there are many degrees" (NA, p. 33).

III

Stevens' limited meaning for "symbolical" offers only a little difficulty. In some of his comments on his poems, his use of the term is especially confusing because it is careless, even inappropriate. His explanation of "Ghosts as Cocoons" speaks of certain phrases intended to be read "literally" and "not so literally" (L, p. 347). But the wording of this poem is figurative: It has only a few literal passages.

The grass is in seed. The young birds are flying.
Yet the house is not built, not even begun.

The vetch has turned purple. But where is the bride?
It is easy to say to those bidden[6]— But where,

Where, butcher, seducer, bloodman, reveller,
Where is sun and music and highest heaven's lust,

For which more than any words cries deeplier?

(CP, p. 119)

Stevens says that "butcher, seducer, etc. is literally the inept politician, and that sort of thing, and again, not quite so literally, evil and unhappiness" (L, p. 347). The literal meaning (but a meaning that is truly figurative) of what mars everything must be interpreted; and Stevens does interpret it when he tells what is figurative. "Butcher, seducer" is a personification of evil and unhappiness, a figure that he describes as not so literal. When Stevens uses the word "literal" he refers to specific images, and by "not so literal" he refers to abstractions. Stevens says that the bride is "literally 'sun and music' etc.; not so literally, love and happiness." Again, interpretation is necessary; for if, as he indicates, the literal meaning is only the figurative language read literally, then it has very little literal sense.

Metonymy dominates Stevens' use of "sun and music" and "highest heaven's lust." Joined, they suggest the idea of a perfection, latent in that it is thought of as desired: a kind of poetry of being "For which more than any words cries deeplier." Sun stands for warmth and brightness, and music for spontaneous feeling, as in his early phrase "music is feeling, then, not sound." "Heaven's lust" implies pleasure in perfection and beauty, forever and ever.

In explanation of two phrases in his poem, Stevens says, " 'Those to be born': 'the grass is in seed': the people of the future who need to know something of the happiness of life." He seems to reveal by this series that these three phrases are equivalent in meaning. But he does not explain some other parts of this poem—for instance, "love being a birth," which may be construed as: Love is born within us just as we ourselves are born into the world, or when we love we are born again as in a spiritual birth.

Stevens' explanation, when enlarged by a careful reading of the poem, indicates that the imperatives in the language of the poem are those of an invocation to an idea of every possible good and every perfection, an idealization ardently desired but never more than a possibility. Since perfection is transcendent, it is only a potential: a ghost that is a cocoon. But because of the fault and flaw and evil present in existence, oncoming generations will despair of finding in their lives perfect love and happiness and will speak of their conception of that longed-for life as "ghost of fragrance falling / On dung." This evil, this "mal," to use Stevens' term of a later date, is intrinsic to existence, and so it prevents future generations from knowing perfection as actuality—from seeing and touching and speaking to the bride. "The fly on the rose prevents us," they would say; "O season / Excelling summer," they would call her. Since the setting of the poem is that of young birds flying and the grass in seed, the season at hand is summer, but the season of the possible presence of the bride is an imagined perfection. Stevens later was to depict several weddings of the imagined and the real, unlike this one in that they are celebrated as occurring.

> She must come now. The grass is in seed and high.
> Come now. Those to be born have need
>
> Of the bride, love being a birth, have need to see
> And to touch her, have need to say to her,
> "The fly on the rose prevents us, O season
> Excelling summer, ghost of fragrance falling
>
> On dung." Come now, pearled and pasted, bloomy-leafed,
> While the domes resound with chant involving chant.
>
> (CP, p. 119)

Stevens remembered that this poem had occurred to him in 1936 during the Great Depression, for in 1940 with World War II already going on he explained that "When *Ghosts* was written there was the same profound desire to be released from all our misfortunes as there is today." Yet the poem itself has more of celebration in it than of despair. It seems to emerge from the feeling of a man who enjoys a perfect summer day and wishes that everyone everywhere could live in a perpetual season of perfect days and perfect happiness.

IV

Stevens' explanation of "The Pleasures of Merely Circulating" is typical of the difficulties to be encountered in reading what he considered clarifications of his poems. He had no intention of offering a plain exegesis, for he said of the little information he did give: "Here again the explanation destroys the poem" (L, p. 348). The poem's major obscurity is due to its ellipses—the gaps in its continuity of meaning. However, his comment does offer a hint of what has been omitted from the discourse.

The first stanza presents the rotation of earth as a natural order imposed on everything earthly, even the products of the human imagination—the idea of the Garden of Paradise and the angel. And because "The angel flew round with the clouds," the clouds belong to the same sphere of the imagined as the angel and, in Stevens' suggestive language, they are thoughts, multitudinous, fluctuating, present in the elevated realm of abstraction where they circulate in possible order or disorder with the basic order of earth's rotation.

> The garden flew round with the angel,
> The angel flew round with the clouds,
> And the clouds flew round and the clouds flew round
> And the clouds flew round with the clouds.
>
> (CP, p. 149)

Stevens begins his explanation of the poem by speaking generally: "The spectacle of order is so vast that it resembles disorder: it resembles the fortuitous." Perhaps the questions of the second stanza suggest that death comes to the living in the natural order of things and holds no secrets and that the supernatural communications longed for by the black-hooded drummers would be a disorder in the natural world if they were more than imagined. The unstated answers to these questions would be no.

> Is there any secret in skulls,
> The cattle skulls in the woods?
> Do the drummers in black hoods
> Rumble anything out of their drums?
>
> (CP, p. 150)

If the answer to these questions should be yes, then the disorder in nature would be such that "Mrs. Anderson's Swedish baby / Might well have been German or Spanish," an irony that turns the reply to the questions back to no. In his letter, Stevens refers pointedly to this stanza when he says, "Swedish babies are as likely as not to be something else" (L, p. 348). This is mere paraphrase, and Stevens is as elliptical here as in his poem. We may understand this couplet as an amusing example of disorder possible only in a world that does not continue its natural order and orderly rotation.

Stevens' comment on the concluding lines—"for all the apparent fortuitousness of things, they hold together"—explains the figurative meaning of "classical." "Yet that things go round and again go round / Has rather a classical sound." The measured recurrence in the line is its "classical sound" in a literal sense. Figuratively, it is a reference to the poet's feeling for the stability and uniformity he finds in the turning of the earth and the assurance of its repetition and succession, which are "classical" because traditional, verifiable.

The title of the poem, "The Pleasures of Merely Circulating," brought into conjunction with the poem may hint that the pleasures are not in the practicing of going up or down, toward heaven or hell, but in merely going round with the natural order of earth. The first stanza illustrates the imagined as circulating with the turning earth. The second stanza questions the ideas that death withholds a secret from the living and that supernatural communication is possible. The third stanza expresses the poet's satisfaction with naturalism.

Stevens' comments on the poem bring into our consideration of its meaning his sense of the vastness of our universe, which is only hinted at in the poem by its playful allusion to the circulation of the imagined in spheres that we create to deal with the incomprehensible. His qualification of the word "disorder" with "resembles" gives emphasis to the surety to be found in the phrase "classical sound." Whatever meaning the poem would convey by itself is affected by his explanation, and the combination of poem and comment gives to this very disjunctive poem a reasonableness whose theme is that our pleasure is in merely circulating in an order so vast that at times it "resembles disorder."

Stevens in his explanation of "The Pleasures of Merely Circulating" is already a "Connoisseur of Chaos." In that later poem,

> A. A violent order is disorder; and
> B. A great disorder is an order. These
> Two things are one.
> (CP, p. 215)

The charm of the early poem depends on the absence of theorizing and the carefree elliptical discourse, and thus it is saved from eclipse by the later, more striking treatment of a similar theme.

NOTES

1. Wallace Stevens, *Letters of Wallace Stevens*, ed. Holly Stevens (New York: Knopf, 1966), p. 293; hereafter cited as L.
2. For extensive examinations of reduction in Stevens see Harold Bloom, *Wallace Stevens: The Poems of Our Climate* (Ithaca, N.Y.: Cornell Univ. Press, 1976), and Thomas J. Hines, *The Later Poetry of Wallace Stevens* (Lewisburgh, Pa.: Bucknell Univ. Press, 1976).
3. Wallace Stevens, *The Collected Poems of Wallace Stevens* (New York: Knopf, 1954), pp. 137–38; hereafter cited as CP.
4. *Opus Posthumous*, ed. Samuel French Morse (New York: Knopf, 1957), p. 184; hereafter cited as OP.
5. Wallace Stevens, *The Necessary Angel* (New York: Knopf, 1951), p. 33; hereafter cited as NA.
6. This line brings to mind the biblical parables of those bidden to a wedding, as in Luke 14.

PETER BRAZEAU

"Hepped on Family Ties":
Wallace Stevens in the 1940s

As Wallace Stevens riffled through his morning mail at the Hartford Accident and Indemnity Company on August 7, 1943, one envelope caught his eye with its unusual code: *S.W.A.K.* In the daily correspondence from field lawyers on bond claim matters or from editors requesting poems for their little magazines, a letter that came *Sealed With A Kiss* stood out. A few nights earlier, four young people had been having a nightcap at a hotel in Reading, Pennsylvania, when the conversation turned to Uncle Wallace in Hartford. In high spirits, his nieces and nephew wrote a community letter filled with family chatter about the new twins and a nephew's promotion to army captain; they also wrote to tell their uncle how often they thought of him and how much they had missed him since his last visit three months earlier, when he had come home to Reading for his sister Elizabeth's interment. "The round-robin has stirred me up considerably," he wrote back immediately. "I am so proud of all of you and so happy to have you think of me that I am not going to allow any dust to gather before I reply."[1] Entering into the game, he dictated a long letter, addressing each relative in turn as if they were still seated next to one another in The Berkshire lounge. When he came to Elizabeth's daughter, Jane, whom he now looked on more as a daughter than a niece, Stevens confided why their note had meant so much to him: "I am a little hepped on family ties. It is one of the sources of strength in life."

Such sentiments are extraordinary when one learns that until quite recently Stevens had stood apart from his family for some twenty-five years. Until his younger brother's funeral a scant three years earlier, Stevens had been only a "strange person off in the distance"[2] to Jane and her cousins who now included Uncle Wallace in their night on the town. Returning to Reading for John Stevens' funeral in the summer of 1940 was one of the emotional and artistic turning points in Stevens' later life as he became a member of the family again after years of separation. The final illness of his older brother, Garrett, in the mid-1930s had led to Stevens' first regular contact with any of his family since his move from New York to Connecticut in 1916, when he joined the Hartford Accident and Indemnity Company. But this was merely a paper tie, a matter of sending money to an ailing and impoverished brother at little personal expense. After years of false starts as a lawyer in Reading, Baltimore, and New York, Garrett had begun to enjoy a promising practice in Cleveland in the 1920s when he was struck with the first of the disabling lung ailments that, along with a heart condition, all but forced him to give up his criminal practice by 1936. He appealed to his financially secure brothers for help, and during the next eighteen months Wallace and John sent several hundred dollars before Garrett's death on November 3, 1937. "At the time of the funeral, Uncle John came but not Wallace," Garrett's daughter remembers. "He wrote, though, and said he was sorry but he just couldn't make it. We thought he would come."[3]

While Stevens had reestablished a modicum of family contact with the monthly checks and notes he had sent Garrett, there was little of the emotional investment or poetic return that came about three years later when he decided to attend the funeral of his last surviving brother, John Stevens, a prominent ex-judge and Democratic party boss of Berks County who had died from ulcer complications on July 9, 1940. Jane MacFarland Wilson recalls the day Uncle Wallace came home again, in every sense of the word, and how it changed their lives—for a time:

> I didn't meet him until I was twenty-one, at the funeral of his younger brother in Reading. I lived in Philadelphia at the time with my mother [Elizabeth], who was in the hospital for a minor operation so she couldn't go. I wasn't really close to the Reading folk: Mother and I had to go up to Reading every Christmas and every Easter, and I was bored stiff. They were just family. Now I was going to a funeral. And I met this gorgeous man who wasn't anything like the Reading folk: he was just delightful.
>
> I know it's true of my mother, she hadn't seen Wallace maybe in twenty-five years. He hadn't seen me or my two cousins which were John's children, and of course there were grandchildren then, too.[4] All this was just like, "Here's my family again after all these years." It really seemed to delight Uncle Wallace. And I think that's what sparked him into researching the family.

Like as not when Mother and I would arrive in Reading and [John's] chauffeur would take us up to the house on Douglass Street, there'd be nobody home. Or Bess, John's wife, would be upstairs sleeping. Or, if John was home, he'd be reading a book or a legal journal, say "Hi, Elizabeth. Hi, Jane," and go back to his reading. It was a strange household; there was a mismatch, too. I thought it unfriendly. When I met Wallace in this atmosphere, he was so human, so warm, that it made more of an impression. There was a chord struck between us almost immediately. My mother used to say that the family just wasn't demonstrative, but she was not that way, and when I would meet Uncle Wallace I would hug and kiss him and he would me. She knew what I felt about the Reading family: "But that's just the way we are, Jane. We've always been that way." And there was a little bit of this in Wallace Stevens, too.

[The day of John's funeral, Stevens] knew my mother was coming home from the hospital to our apartment in Germantown. He said, "Well, I think I'll return home with you. I haven't seen Elizabeth in all this time; I would like to see her." [Coming] into the apartment, I said "Mother, guess what? I've brought Uncle Wallace home." So the first time he's seen her now in twenty-five years, he looks at her and says, "My God, Elizabeth, you've put it on!" My mother was a tremendous person: she was six-two and weighed two hundred and fifty. But there he was sticking out like that, too. She was pretty fast on the uptake, so I'm sure she said [something back]. They got on real fine after that. From then on he replaced what John had been to her. If there were financial difficulties John helped her out. Then it became Wallace. He was very generous. He helped me more than once, not just financially, after my mother died. . . . [After Wallace's reunion with Elizabeth] they wrote, but I wouldn't say a heavy correspondence. I don't think she ever became very interested [in genealogy], but he kept after people because now he was becoming very interested and had her look up people like Emma Jobbins [a first cousin who knew a good deal about family history] and some other remote cousins in the out-towns of Pennsylvania to see what they might have or who Wallace could contact.

Now I'm not an egghead, but I got so full of myself for thinking that I could understand some of *Harmonium*, I talked to him finally about it. In the thirties, John [Stevens] received a copy. He said, "What's this? I can't understand this kind of stuff!" They made much about "What's all this?" So I picked up the book and I did understand it. [Later, Jane talked to Stevens about his poetry.] "Is this what you meant?" His answer on one occasion was, "Well, I might have meant that at one time. I don't know what I meant now." I kind of believe that. He may have written things that later on he couldn't interpret. His later poetry I could no longer keep in touch with, and I told him, "I used to understand but now I don't. Or at least, I think I understood. I liked to read it. It does something for me, but now I've lost it." So he stopped sending me books in the fifties. It didn't affect our relationship in any way; our relationship was entirely different. This may be an indication. One time after my divorce [in 1945] I came up to Philadelphia to visit my friends. And Wallace and I planned to meet in New York. He took me to lunch at the Waldorf Astoria and then to see *Bloomer Girl*. He loved it; I loved it. Ours was a very light thing; we never got into the deep things. This was probably relaxation for him, and he knew I enjoyed it. And he did too, wholeheartedly.

When my mother died, which was February 1943, he was the one I turned to. I called and he came down [to Philadelphia]. He made all the arrangements. He stayed with me. [He acted] very warmly. I can remember the day of the funeral. He said, "Now, let's get out; it's a beautiful day." [On a winter's afternoon in Philadelphia] you'd think it would be miserable, but the sun was shining, it was warm. We walked along the Parkway and walked along Chestnut Street, downtown Philadelphia. We looked in this [bakery] window, and they had a whiskey cake there. He said, "Oh, I bet that's delightful. Now tomorrow you get one and have one sent to me." He loved good-tasting things. He said, "Now you're not alone. You've got me." And I had him. I loved him. I had a father that was never really my father [her parents having been divorced when she was a child]. That's what Wallace took on for me, the father image, at that time.

I knew Wallace in the last fifteen years of his life, and it was the best thing that had happened to me up to that point. I swear it was love at first sight at that funeral because going down on that train to see my mother, he said, "You seem so much more like a Stevens than any of the Stevenses here." And I thought, "That's just great. I really made it now."

Wallace Stevens soon grew curious about precisely what it meant to be a Stevens. He began his research casually enough in the summer of 1941, asking the Daughters of the American Revolution, for example, about the ancestral information his mother had submitted when she had applied for membership years earlier. This curiosity about his elders, however, soon turned into the obsession it remained through most of the 1940s. A common interest in genealogy, in fact, provided one of the few topics of conversation between Elsie and Wallace Stevens in later years. She had become interested in her ancestry even earlier than her husband when she had applied for D.A.R. membership in the late 1930s. Her interest may well have helped to arouse his own. Stevens' initial curiosity about older generations, however, may owe at least as much to his visits with the younger generation of Stevenses, visits that preseded his first genealogical inquiries that summer of 1941.

In the months following John's funeral in the summer of 1940, Stevens not only took the trouble to return to Reading for a nephew's wedding but also had come to enjoy the company of his nieces and nephews so much that he invited John Stevens, Jr., and his bride to visit him at Westerly Terrace and invited Jane to spend nothing less than an unheard of week as a guest at his Hartford home. In the company of this young family, for now only his sister and Garrett's widow survived from his generation, Stevens had come back home as the family patriarch. Finding himself at sixty in this new role may well have helped turn Stevens' thoughts to the elders who had once occupied the position in the family that he now held. As he later explained, "My grandparents, Benjamin Stevens and Elizabeth Barcalow, were like figures in an idyll to me. When I was a boy my father took me down from Reading to the farm at Feasterville to visit them occasionally. It was my remembrance of them that interested me in finding out about their own parents and grandparents."[5]

No one was more surprised than Stevens, however, at how quickly this curiosity grew into an obsession. "Who could ever have imagined that, after three or four years, I should still be at work on this," he wrote to a cousin in 1945,[6] unaware that he would still be at work on his family tree at the end of the decade. It was a task on which he spent hundreds of hours and thousands of dollars. Over a third of Stevens' voluminous archive—some 2,500 items in the form of letters, documents, and his multivolume "work-in-progress" as he called his family history of the Stevens, Zeller, and Barcalow lines—testifies to this passion. The energy he expended on this genealogical enterprise makes the question of what got him started in the summer of 1941 pale when one asks what made him persist so intently throughout the decade when either of his other tasks might well have occupied the full-time attention of a man in his sixties. He not only continued to head the surety claim department of a national insurance company during this period but also increased his output as a man of letters, becoming active as a lecturer as well as a poet.

When his mother had become interested in her ancestry years earlier and had sought to join the Daughters of the American Revolution, young Stevens had sneered at her motives as simple snobbery. Yet there was certainly an element of snobbery in his own research even if in his egalitarian moods he asserted, "after muddling round with American genealogy for several years, I think that a decent sort of carpenter, or a really robust blacksmith, or a woman capable of having eleven sons and of weaving their clothes and the blankets under which they slept, and so on, is certainly no less thrilling" than finding more notable connections.[7] While Stevens claimed he was content to find that his ancestry was decidedly plebeian, he remained intensely disappointed that his research did not make him eligible for membership in an exclusive New York genealogical society, which would have bolstered his claim to a distinguished Dutch-American pedigree. He wanted very much to belong to the Holland Society, he confided to Lila James Roney, the genealogist who worked full-time for two years on his family lines until her death in 1944: "when I start to talk about being descended from the first white child born in New Netherland, people who wouldn't believe it otherwise would believe it if I could say that I was a member of the Holland Society."[8]

At best, his research only qualified him for the less prestigious St. Nicholas Society. In "Recitation after Dinner," the poem he wrote in 1945 for that society's annual banquet, however, Stevens described a far more profound impulse than simple snobbery that was at the heart of some of his most intense efforts to uncover his ancestral ties:

> That of the son who bears upon his back
> The father that he loves, and bears him from
> The ruins of the past, out of nothing left,
> Made noble by the honor he receives,
> As if in a golden cloud. The son restores
> The father.[9]

One of his earliest family lyrics shows that from the beginning of the 1940s this sense of filial devotion as much as family vanity started Stevens looking backward for a decade. In March 1942, six months after his earliest extant genealogical query, he published "Outside of

Wedlock" in *Trend*. Here, as in later family poems, Stevens did not boast of his pedigree or mythologize his ancestors' era as a golden age. Instead he commanded the winter wind, that bleakest sound in his work, to sing a dirge, as if it spoke with the voice of his Dutch Adam and Eve, Benjamin and Blandenah:

> Sing . . .
> White February wind,
> Through banks and banks of voices,
> In the cathedral-shanty,
>
> To the sound of the concertina,
> Like the voice of all our ancestors,
> The *père* Benjamin, the *mère* Blandenah,
> Saying we have forgot them, they never lived.
>
> (OP, p. 77)

Yet the poem itself does not, like the wind's song within it, simply mourn the oblivion of Benjamin and Blandenah's generation and, by implication, the oblivion of each succeeding generation including Stevens'. By remembering his ancestors with this filial poem, Stevens alters their fate, brings them back to life—on paper at least.

Nowhere is Stevens more strikingly the Dutch Aeneas of "Recitation after Dinner" than in his dogged efforts to bear his great-grandfather, John Zeller, the most prominent family member in his poetry, out of the most profound obscurity. At the same time, "The Bed of Old John Zeller," published as his three-year search for his ancestor was ending in the fall of 1944, offers an interesting glimpse into the way genealogical research translated itself into poetry. On April 14, 1943, a year and a half after he had begun to inquire about the Zellers, his mother's side of the family, Stevens complained how frustrated he was. While Lila Roney, his full-time genealogist, had already traced his father's line as far back as the first settlers of New Netherland, the part-time genealogist, Mary Owen Steinmetz, who had worked for months in Reading on the Zellers had not been able to tell him even the name of his mother's grandfather. "This man's line is the only one in the family on which I cannot even get started,"[10] he wrote in exasperation to a minister in Reading, hoping his church records might offer some clues about his grandfather's parentage. Stevens planned to visit Reading a few weeks later when the minister would officiate at his sister Elizabeth's interment in the family plot, Elizabeth having died in Philadelphia in late winter. That first weekend in May, Stevens made a visit home to his relatives, one of the half-dozen he made between 1940 and 1945, the period of his closest ties to the younger generation. He visited Reading infrequently, partly because of the difficulties of wartime travel, but he did come home for family occasions—weddings, funerals, and wartime reunions with furloughed relatives—that bind a family closer. Once he had become interested in his genealogy, however, he also looked forward to these trips to Pennsylvania because they were opportunities to strengthen his ancestral ties, which he did on this spring visit.

That weekend, Stevens made the breakthrough about his great-grandfather he had hoped for. He learned from a memorandum the minister wrote that his grandfather had been John Zeller, Jr.; in the family parlance, then, his great-grandfather had been Old John Zeller, as Stevens referred to him in his poem the following year. It took that year for Stevens to piece his great-grandfather's identity together. "Genealogy has become a sort of substitute for the reading of detective stories,"[11] he wrote a nephew in the autumn of 1944 when the puzzle was almost complete. Born during the Revolutionary War, Old John Zeller spent his boyhood on a farm in the Tulpehocken area of Berks County, Pennsylvania, where his own great-grandfather, the original Zeller immigrant, had settled in the 1720s, some years after coming to America. As a young man, John and his wife, Catherine, left the farm for Philadelphia, where he learned the shoemaking trade which he later taught one of his sons. (Wallace Stevens' mother, a woman of social pretensions, insisted that her father was not a simple shoemaker but a maker of fine boots.) John Zeller soon returned home from Philadelphia and bought a small farm in Stevens' beloved Oley Valley, not far from Reading, where he lived out his seventy-nine years until his death in 1858. All these details were important to Stevens the genealogist. At the time, however, they meant little to Stevens the poet in characterizing his great-grandfather in "The Bed of Old John Zeller," where he figures prominently.

In this poem Stevens describes his great-grandfather in terms of a certain cast of mind. "the habit of wishing, as if one's grandfather lay / In one's heart and wished as he had always wished."[12] In fact, nothing in Stevens' research regarding this ancestor had uncovered anything specific about the man's way of thinking. Rather, in defining him as he did in the poem Stevens drew on his sense of the Zeller line generally. Old John Zeller stands not so much as an individual as a member of the family, and for Stevens the essential feature of the Zeller family was its religious cast of mind, which he judges in this lyric to be a form of wishful thinking. At the time he wrote this poem, for example, most likely spring–summer 1944, Stevens characterized the family in which Old John Zeller had grown up by its religious frame of mind. This family "seems to have been both poor and pious. But I cannot say that the family was poor because I really know nothing about it."[13] Though he admitted he knew little else about that Zeller generation, retracting even his statement that they were poor as soon as he made it, it is not surprising that he did not qualify his assertion that they were pious. For Stevens, a fervent habit of mind was what struck him most about the Zellers from their beginnings in America. "These people, whatever else they were, were fanatics" (L, p. 534), he decided about the original immigrants. One senses his particular association of the Zellers with a zealous religious attitude when one contrasts this remark with his view of the state of mind of the original Dutch immigrants on his father's side. "I don't believe they came out for the purpose of being alone with their maker" since "the Dutch did not come to this country for political and religious freedom . . . the settlement of New Amsterdam was almost wholly a money-making scheme to the Dutch."[14]

Recognizing Stevens' close identification of the Zellers with a devoutly pious habit of mind helps to gloss the key middle section of "The Bed of Old John Zeller":

> This is the habit of wishing, as if one's grandfather lay
> In one's heart and wished as he had always wished, unable
>
> To sleep in that bed for its disorder, talking of ghostly
> Sequences that would be sleep and ting-tang tossing, so that
> He might slowly forget. It is more difficult to evade
>
> That habit of wishing and to accept the structure
> Of things as the structure of ideas.
> (CP, p. 327)

Genealogy provided Stevens with a particularly witty way to describe the supernatural yearnings that occasionally stirred in his secular heart when he confronted the meaning of the natural world: They are, here, the fitful tossings of an insomniac ancestor. By identifying this ancestor as a Zeller in his title, Stevens wryly indictes the strength of these bouts, for a Zeller would be particularly uncomfortable in the presence of such secular disorder and would be given to a good deal of tossing about. Further, by tracing these stirrings to the Zeller line, whose piety Stevens once described as fanatical, the genealogical figure accounts for such traditional attitudes surviving fitfully within the poet even at this late date. Finally, the identification of this ancestor as a Zeller explains the difficulty Stevens their descendant had in evading such a response, as it were, given the tenacity with which the Zellers held their religious views.

The metaphor of the bed in this conceit grew out of Stevens' search for the actual resting place of Old John Zeller during the spring and summer of 1944. In late May, by pure chance, his Reading genealogist happened upon a reference to the elusive grave while leafing through a volume containing tombstone inscriptions from a country churchyard in Amityville, Pennsylvania, a few miles from Reading. During the next few months, while Stevens was intent on locating the actual site in the churchyard where his great-grandfather lay, he imagined for a moment that he lay much closer to home, another metamorphosis of genealogical research into poetry.

In the autumn of 1944, as "The Bed of Old John Zeller" was being published in *Accent,* Stevens received word that Zeller's actual resting place had been located. Though Zeller had died only twenty-one years before Stevens' birth and had been buried only a few miles from the town where Stevens had grown up, the proximity but elusiveness of the grave suggested how quickly one could be forgotten by the family, how quickly one could suffer the same fate as the more remote Benjamin and Blandenah. The marker had fallen to the ground, where it lay untended, the name on the dilapidated stone hidden beneath moss and vines. The description of complete neglect that the pastor of the church, Dr. Howard Althouse, sent when he located the grave in late September spoke eloquently of the fate of Stevens' ancestors which, as "Outside of Wedlock" shows, touched the poet deeply from the outset of his research. In early October, Stevens set about having the site restored and the stones reset.

It is an apt gesture with which to end this discussion of the ancestral ties Stevens wove in the 1940s, dramatizing Stevens' Virgilian sense of his role as family historian, in this instance literally bearing his ancestor out of the ruins of the past. Weaving such ties was, of course, also psychically self-serving. An old man himself at the time, Stevens was Anchises as well as Aeneas. His ancestors were his surrogates. Rescuing them from oblivion, either on paper or where they lay, Stevens was reassuring himself. Family ties were life lines that reached in both directions.

NOTES

1. Unpublished letter to Eleanor Sauer et al. at the Huntington Library, Art Gallery and Botanical Garden, to which I am grateful for permission to quote from this and from

all unpublished letters cited below.

2. Taped interview with Jane MacFarland Wilson.

3. Taped interview with Mary Catharine Sesnick.

4. There seems to have been little contact between Stevens and his sister during the twenty-five years prior to his spur-of-the-moment visit to her home after their brother's funeral in the summer of 1940. While Stevens apparently wrote to Elizabeth twice in May 1919, after her daughter Jane's birth early that month and after their sister Mary Katharine's death at the end of the month, the only extant correspondence between them during these years is a postcard Elizabeth sent to him from Tokyo when she was on vacation in 1931 and a check for $75 that he sent her in the spring of 1940, a few months before their reunion. Stevens' daughter, Holly, has some recollection that as a child she met her aunt, perhaps when Elizabeth was working as a dietician at a Girl Scout camp in Brandford, Connecticut, during the summer of 1933 and made a day trip to Hartford with friends to see the sights. In the long letter Elizabeth wrote to her daughter at the time, detailing the day's experiences, however, she makes no mention of seeing her brother Wallace or his family.

   Stevens may have met his brother John's children earlier; some family members recalled that Stevens was at the Reading funeral of John's wife, Elizabeth, in the mid-1930s. Nonetheless, Jane Wilson is correct that the renewed relationship between Stevens and his Pennsylvania family dates from his pivotal meeting with them when he returned home for John's funeral in 1940.

5. Undated memorandum at the Huntington Library, Art Gallery and Botanical Garden.

6. Unpublished letter to Emma Jobbins, 19 February 1945.

7. Unpublished letter to W. N. P. Dailey, 16 May 1945.

8. Unpublished letter, 25 August 1944.

9. Wallace Stevens, *Opus Posthumous*, ed. Samuel French Morse (New York: Knopf, 1957), p. 87; hereafter cited as OP.

10. Unpublished memorandum to Dr. Campbell.

11. Unpublished letter to John C. Sauer, 3 October, 1944.

12. Wallace Stevens, *The Collected Poems of Wallace Stevens* (New York: Knopf, 1954), p. 327; hereafter cited as CP.

13. Wallace Stevens, *Letters of Wallace Stevens*, ed. Holly Stevens (New York: Knopf, 1966), p. 470; hereafter cited as L.

14. Unpublished letter to Lila James Roney, 4 October 1943.

ROBERT BUTTEL

The Incandescence of Old Age:
Yeats and Stevens in
Their Late Poems

"Bodily decrepitude is wisdom," asserts W. B. Yeats in the well-known aphorism in "After Long Silence." His three old Chinamen in "Lapis Lazuli" are embodiments of that wisdom, achieving as they move up the mountain a state of sublimity, of serene transcendence. Surveyors of the earthly and tragic scene below, they manifest a state of grace; they are alive, enriched by their long years of human experience, while at the same time they enjoy an unearthly perspective. It is a state of blessedness similar to that which Yeats reported having experienced himself, though such occasions were probably infrequent given the poet's restive spirit and his awareness of the difficulty for humans in reaching states of perfection, of harmonious being. He reports one instance in the final stanza of "A Dialogue of Self and Soul":

> I am content to follow to its source
> Every event in action or in thought;
> Measure the lot; forgive myself the lot!
> When such as I cast out remorse
> So great a sweetness flows into the breast
> We must laugh and we must sing,
> We are blest by everything,
> Everything we look upon is blest.[1]

In a later instance, in poem IV of "Vacillation," when his "fiftieth year had come and gone," the ecstatic seizure is more sudden, more dramatic:

> While on the shop and street I gazed
> My body of a sudden blazed;

And twenty minutes more or less
It seemed, so great my happiness,
That I was blessèd and could bless.
                    (WBY, p. 246)

Wallace Stevens, a poet radically different from Yeats in most ways, presents in "Credences of Summer" an image of sublime fulfillment that is very like the state epitomized by Yeats' Chinamen. Stevens refers to "the natural tower of all the world" and to "the refuge that the end creates." Here the radiance of an absolute, the sun seen without metaphor, without evasion, is symbolized (in a characteristic sleight-of-hand use of metaphor) as

> . . . the old man standing on the tower,
> Who reads no book. His ruddy ancientness
> Absorbs the ruddy summer and is appeased,
> By an understanding that fulfils his age,
> By a feeling capable of nothing more.[2]

And Stevens, like Yeats, arrives at more intimate and personal realizations of superior consciousness, of blessedness—or, as he puts it in "The Auroras of Autumn"—of holiness. It is "An innocence of earth." In order

> That we partake thereof,
> Lie down like children in this holiness,
> As if, awake, we lay in the quiet of sleep.
>   (CP, p. 418)

In "A Quiet Normal Life" the epiphany is characterized, as in Yeats' "Vacillation," by a blazing. "In his chair," the speaker tells us, "the most tranquil thought grew peaked." Then after a disclaimer—"There was no fury in transcendent forms" (but how often for Yeats there was!) — the poem concludes: "But his actual candle blazed with artifice."

Despite his many differences from Yeats and the above disclaimer, Stevens also conceived a "fury" at the center of things. "The Motive for Metaphor," for instance, is a

> shrinking from
> The weight of primary noon,
> The A B C of being,

The ruddy temper, the hammer
Of red and blue, the hard sound —
Steel against intimation—the sharp flash,
The vital, arrogant, fatal, dominant X.

(CP, p. 288)

These lines project a humanly uninhabitable and terrifying center of being, of reality, where inhuman force exists. X marks its inescapable existence but at the same time is a sign of its ultimate unknowability. For Yeats the human encounter with this inhuman, supernatural dimension produces a shattering apocalyptic moment of beauty and terror. Stevens, in "Prologues to What Is Possible," entertains the possibility of such an encounter as the speaker describes in a strange, dreamlike metaphor a mystical voyage into the center of some ultimate meaning. But arrival at that meaning would "shatter the boat" and leave the oarsmen cut off from humanity: "Removed from any shore, from any man or woman, and needing none." Even as he faced the impossibility of actually penetrating the unknown and gaining a knowledge of the absolute, however, Stevens yearned for the consolations of myth, desiring, like Yeats, fulfillment, order, and certainty; hence he envisioned "A larger poem for a larger audience, / As if the crude collops came together as one, / A mythological form" (Canto I, "An Ordinary Evening in New Heaven"). To the end, both poets persist in reaching for what Stevens referred to as "the inhuman more" (Section VIII, "The Sail of Ulysses")—indeed the achievement of their late poems depends greatly on that continued reaching. At supreme moments each brings the known and unknown into conjunction. In the symbolic refrain of "Long-Legged Fly," for example, Yeats brings human time and the flow of history into a preternatural union with the eternal: *"Like a long-legged fly upon the stream / His mind moves upon silence."* The effect is spectral, trancelike. Stevens, in "The River of Rivers in Connecticut," similarly brings the particular, physical phenomenon ("The steeple at Farmington" which "Stands glistening" as "Haddam shines and sways") into a transcendent identity with the universal river, "an unnamed flowing, / Space-filled, reflecting the seasons, the folk-lore / Of each of the senses, . . . The river that flows nowhere, like a sea."

But perhaps what makes the late poems of these two poets so compelling is that their stance toward mortality and the diminishment of powers tends to be unaccommodated, taken without the comforting mediation of myth or religion. They both come finally to confront extinction with few if any defenses between their own consciousness and this abyss, and from this confrontation they extract their final poems, bringing the techniques of their long careers to an exquisite economy, gathering thought and emotion into a tight circle of the essential, wherein they are most expressive and most controlled, most stringent and most powerful, most austere and most noble.

I have called attention to these areas of convergence because the points of divergence are much more apparent. Yeats is passionate, dramatic, oracular, apocalyptic, and concerned with history, for example, while Stevens, increasingly in his later poetry, is meditative, speculative, quietly metaphysical, and attuned to the transient moment in nature. A list of differences would only begin here. To conceive how far apart these two poets are in most ways (no matter how much Stevens must have admired the work of the Irish poet) one has only to imagine the improbable consequences of a meeting and conversation between them: Such a conversation would strain the resources even of a Walter Savage Landor's imagination. Yet both poets pursued their calling with a continuing growth of mastery into their seventies and up to their deaths. They were both in their differing ways, and stretching the term only slightly, religious poets for whom the consolations of formal religion had ceased to exist. Poetry should help us to live our lives, Stevens claimed. Hence the responses to the fate of old age and mortality by these two major modern poets in the poems they wrote toward the ends of their lives ought to be of more than mere literary interest.

If for Yeats old age brought wisdom, the thought of death evoked both panic and attraction; he was drawn again and again to those moments of death and transfiguration that were so integral to his complex of history, myth, and self, and much of the power of his work derives from his yearning to transcend death and bodily decrepitude. The point at which life and death, the temporal and the supernatural, impinge stirred in Yeats his most characteristic stances and emotions—strange emotions, frequently combining terror and trance or a giddy gaiety. Those men who in "Vacillation" ". . . come / Proud, open-eyed and laughing to the tomb" would seem to arrive there in a somewhat manic, possessed state. The two earlier Byzantium poems, of course, represent a more intense, more extreme solution to the duality of life and death, of body and soul: the escape from the body in a scene of ecstatic supernatural mystery so as to achieve, in the imagination at least, absorption into "the artifice of eternity," in effect a personal apotheosis. What Geoffrey Hartmann says of Keats' odes—that they "are a feverish quest to enter the life of a pictured scene, to be totally where the imagination is"— can be said also of "Sailing to Byzantium" and "Byzantium." How human by comparison is Crazy Jane's devotion to the body as well as to the soul. In Crazy Jane, Yeats lit upon a brilliantly apt persona, not only for conveying his conception of unified being but also for the wisdom that erupts with half-crazed, wild clairvoyance and the authority of an old crone interpreting life from the perspective of one near death.

Last Poems, however, more definitely anticipate the end. In part there is a summing up, as in "The Municipal Gallery Revisited" and "Beautiful Lofty Things," poems that celebrate and glory in the friends Yeats has had, or in "Under Ben Bulben," in which he accepts and prepares for death and offers a kind of last will and testament for the Irish poets to come. The latter poem not only concludes with its ceremonious elegy for self and directions for the portentous words to be cut on his gravestone (right to the end he was capable of posturing) but also contains some rather easy words about death: "Many times man lives and dies / Between his two eternities" and "A brief parting from those dear / Is the worst man has to fear." In this valedictory poem such sentiments are understandable. Much more compelling, however, are those poems in which Yeats allows himself little if any solace as he faces the desperation of the end. In these he bursts out with feelings of fear, of frenzy, of indignation, of anguish. "Why Should Not Old Men Be Mad?" asks the title of one poem, which cites sardonically the follies, injustices, and tragic perversity of life that "Observant old men know . . . well." Even when a sense of accomplishment and fulfillment is realized at the end of life in "What Then?" the chilling question reverberates: "'What then!' sang Plato's ghost. 'What then!' " And the tension between life and death produced in the final stanza of "The Apparitions" reaches an extreme:

> When a man grows old his joy
> Grows more deep day after day,
> His empty heart is full at length,
> But he has need of all that strength
> Because of the increasing Night
> That opens her mystery and fright.
> *Fifteen apparitions have I seen;*
> *The worst a coat upon a coat-hanger.*
> (WBY, p. 332)

It is a delirious, precarious balance here, with the joy all but swallowed in the panic that arises at the thought of the opening abyss.

The awareness of impending annihilation charges the last poems with their furious energy. In them Yeats would extract from the very desperateness of his condition his final aesthetic triumphs. As he asks in "The Spur," "What else have I [but "lust and rage"] to spur me into song?" And in "An Acre of Grass" he calls for "an old man's frenzy," which will enable him to "remake" himself so that, like Timon, Lear, Blake, and Michelangelo, he can with his "old man's eagle mind" pierce through the limitations of old age and mortality to an absolute knowledge—a knowledge of human limitation and human glory brought at the point of personal extinction into a union of utmost intensity. Yeats' histrionic stances themselves become part of the transmogrifying intensity of these last poems, in which posturing carried somehow beyond posturing. The old poet certainly assumes a self-regarding stance in "The Circus Animals' Desertion" as he thinks back on his "old themes" and "masterful images," which "Grew in pure mind," but the unflinching bitter recognition at the end, as he admits the disgusting source of his images, manages to ennoble the stance; his acceptance of the fate of flesh and mortality avoids self-pity: ". . . Now that my ladder's gone, / I must lie down where all the ladders start, / In the foul rag-and-bone shop of the heart."

In contrast is Stevens' view as he thinks back on some of his major poems and themes, in one of his last poems, "As You Leave the Room":

> *You speak. You say:* Today's character is not
> A skeleton out of its cabinet. Nor am I.
>
> That poem about the pineapple, the one
> About the mind as never satisfied,
>
> The one about the credible hero, the one
> About summer, are not what skeletons think about.[3]

But then he wonders, has he after all

> lived a skeleton's life,
> As a disbeliever in reality,
>
> A countryman of all the bones in the world?
>
> (OP, p. 117)

How calm, how reflective is his wondering. No tortured recognition of his mortal, physical being, no bitter disgust as he considers the potential futility of his endeavors, no horror in his reference to a skeleton in a cabinet (compare the tone here with Yeats' agitation over the empty coat on a hanger in "The Apparitions"). Indeed, the response to his question, as he becomes mindful of the actual day, is a modest assertion of the present moment's value:

> Now, here, the snow I had forgotten becomes
>
> Part of a major reality . . .
>
> And thus an elevation, as if I left
> With something I could touch, touch every way.
>
> And yet nothing has been changed except what is
> Unreal, as if nothing had been changed at all.
>
> (OP, p. 117)

Necessary, then, to this fresh apprehension of reality and the resulting elevation is a purging of the unreal. Hence the momentary sense of intimate human contact: "something I could touch, touch every way." Affecting the poignance of this elevation is the subtle intimation of the title, "As You Leave the Room," hinting at this point in the poet's life at final departure. In the poem "Long and Sluggish Lines" the fact of aging is associated with boredom: "It makes so little difference, at so much more / Than seventy, where one looks, one has been there before." But this attitude is superseded by a realization of life breaking through:

> . . . these—escent—issant pre-personae: first fly,
> A comic infanta among the tragic drapings,
>
> Babyishness of forsythia, a snatch of belief,
> The spook and makings of the nude magnolia . . .
>
> (CP, p. 522)

In Stevens' end are these beginnings, returns to the now, to "an always incipient cosmos" ("July Mountain"). Even when Stevens considers the possibility of some ultimate meaning, as in "Prologues to What Is Possible," he in effect draws back from what would be an obliterating experience. But just to contemplate such an absolute, transcendent fulfillment seems to suffice for the discovery of new selves. And a "flick" of transcendent knowledge seems to remain, enough to transform the perception of reality:

A flick which added to what was real and its vocabulary,
The way some first thing coming into Northern trees
Adds to them the whole vocabulary of the South,
The way the earliest single light in the evening sky, in spring,
Creates a fresh universe out of nothingness by adding itself,
The way a look or a touch reveals its unexpected magnitudes.

(CP, p. 517)

Thus he is brought back to reality and to the human but with a heightened consciousness.

Stevens attributes such a heightened consciousness to George Santayana in "To an Old Philosopher in Rome." Stevens describes him hovering on the threshold between the earthly Rome "and that more merciful Rome / Beyond, the two alike in the make of the mind." The old philosopher exemplifies "The human end in the spirit's greatest reach, / The extreme of the known in the presence of the extreme / Of the unknown"; Santayana is "alive / Yet living in two worlds." In this moving tribute Santayana comes as close to sanctification as is possible in Stevens' scheme of things, and thus he achieves "a kind of total grandeur at the end," the "grandeur of a total edifice," which amounts to the fully realized form of the self, as though in the rarified nature of his thought he had created the completed poem of his existence (like Stevens himself, he is "an inquisitor of structures"). Such fulfillment, however, Stevens makes clear, arises out of human need and an awareness of mortality. Santayana, says Stevens, is

Impatient for the grandeur that you need

In so much misery, and yet finding it
Only in misery, the afflatus of ruin,
Profound poetry of the poor and of the dead,
As in the last drop of the deepest blood,
As it falls from the heart and lies there to be seen.

(CP, p.509)

"This," says Stevens, "is the tragic accent of the scene."

If we return to the last stanza of Yeats' "The Apparitions," we see a similar formulation but in Yeatsian terms, with all the differences that implies:

When a man grows old his joy
Grows more deep day after day,

His empty heart is full at length,
But he has need of all that strength
Because of the increasing Night
That opens her mystery and fright.

(WBY, p. 332)

Yeats is *in* the tragic scene; we feel that the terror is actual. Stevens, though, ponders the scene. His emotions are engaged by the *idea* of the tragic and by the nobility and fulfillment that Santayana represents; these are exquisite emotions, but they lack the emotional immediacy that Yeats presents. Yeats catches us up in the vehement personal drama of old age and death; Stevens moves us quietly with poignant philosophical meditation. Stevens seems to accept nature as providential, and ideally observes it with calm delight right at the threshold of what lies beyond. For Yeats the knowledge "There on the edges of oblivion"—to use Stevens' phrase in "The Owl in the Sarcophagus" — arrives with fantastic intensity: "Black out; Heaven blazing into the head: / Tragedy wrought to its uttermost" ("Lapis Lazuli"). For Yeats the edges are clear-cut, and, he wrests meaning from despair by a defiant act of will. For Stevens the edges are less sharply defined, and the effect of his last poems is like that of a valedictory note held—the sadness of departure mingled with a reverence for and delight in the constant renewal in nature. If his last poems lack the dramatic intensity of Yeats' last poems, they offer other satisfactions. In them the idea of death as the mother of beauty assumes its own quiet intensity of effect, for death becomes also the mother of a knowledge fully tested in contemplation and accepted with a grace of human feeling. It is a knowledge of the limits of knowledge and of being human, and it requires an acceptance of hovering on the edge of knowing and not knowing, aware of a dimension almost palpable but beyond human grasp. To exist in a bronze perfection, however desirable, would be impossible, but the recognition of that impossibility returns one to the now fresh again phenomenal world and a savoring of the preciousness of existence. In this way the late poems capture the elusive essence of being. They become autumnal distillations of a mind, a sensibility, that discovers unpredictable instants of fulfillment in seemingly simple and ordinary manifestations of nature, as in the "scrawny cry" in "Not Ideas about the Thing But the Thing Itself."

Yeats, of course, would crash through earthly limitations into what I have referred to as a personal apotheosis. In "The Statesman's Holiday" we find, if not apotheosis, something like it. In this poem he sets against the nostalgic contrapuntal refrain —*"Tall dames go walking in grass-*

green Avalon"—his persona's cynical rejection of the modern world and its lack of aristocratic values. The persona has taken up the trade of singing and has become a poor romantic vagabond accompanying himself on "a Montenegrin lute" with "its old sole string." In the third and final stanza, however, Yeats with a mastery of technique wrenches the point of view to third-person description of a cocky artist-outcast:

> With boys and girls about him,
> With any sort of clothes,
> With a hat out of fashion,
> With old patched shoes,
> With a ragged bandit cloak,
> With an eye like a hawk,
> With a stiff straight back
> With a strutting turkey walk,
> With a bag full of pennies,
> With a monkey on a chain,
> With a great cock's feather,
> With an old foul tune.
> *Tall dames go walking in grass-green Avalon.*
>
> (WBY, p. 334)

Here frustration and defiance are transformed into mad triumph. Yeats avoids a potentially sentimental depiction of the organ grinder as the alienated hero-artist by the syntactical daring of the series of "With" phrases (their tension heightened by the very piling up without completion), by the tightly controlled extravagant energy of the rhythm, and by the stretching to the limit of the counterpoint between the refrain and the image of the bizarre figure with his "old foul tune." With the shift in point of view and these other strategies, Yeats transfigures what would be merely a trite poetic archetype. The figure is distanced, larger than life, and at the same time vivid, particular, immediate. In this figure is all the psychic energy of Yeats' own feelings about artist and society—his resentment, bitterness, and proud conviction of art's timeless value. All this he would fix in an absolute, immutable image. For him it was important that his poems survive as though their words were carved in stone.

For Stevens "It was not important that" his poems "survive."

> What mattered was that they should bear
> Some lineament or character,
>
> Some affluence, if only half-perceived,

In the poverty of their words,
Of the planet of which they were part.
(CP, pp. 532-33)

Fittingly, the persona in this poem, "The Planet on the Table," is Ariel, a mercurial, evanescent spirit, now here, now gone. Stevens was more content with the transient, and his style, in contradistinction to Yeats', seems to ride on an air of improvisation. Alert to the changes in nature, he registers epiphanies as they occur in matter-of-fact situations, as in his poem "On the Way to the Bus," wherein "A light snow, like frost, has fallen during the night." Out of this comes

A perception of cold breath, more revealing than
A perception of sleep, more powerful

Than a power of sleep, a clearness emerging
From cold, slightly irised, slightly bedazzled,

But a perfection emerging from a new known,
An understanding beyond journalism.
(OP, p.116)

Like Yeats, Stevens knows that we live in a bad time (indeed, "In a Bad Time" is the title of one of his late poems), but he manages to discover a redemptive meaning in nature beyond the banal understanding of journalism. Yeats, however, redeems his despair by subjecting his dramatic sense of self to the utmost aesthetic pressure, to the exacting demands of his technique, and thus transmutes his passion into indelible form. The poems of these two poets, then, create radically different effects. I believe, however, that the respective pleasures one derives are equal in value and that both poets in their different ways help us to live our lives.

Alain Renais' film *Providence* concerns an aging writer in the throes of a terminal disease, probably cancer. For most of the film we see him proud, defiant, at times bitter or struck by fear, raging against his bodily failings and the approach of death, almost maniacally determined to complete the novel he is working on. In this way he is, of course, most like Yeats. The final scene, however, is a farewell meal with members of his family, set outside his Victorian mansion, on a lawn that sweeps away from the house toward groves of trees and beyond them to a panorama of rolling, wooded hills. The atmosphere as the day ends is serene, idyllic; we feel the writer's attachment to what is spread around him: life and nature, "acutest at [their] vanishing," to use a phrase from "The Idea of Order at Key West." The camera pans the scene as lovingly as a camera can, and then we sense, as Stevens puts it in "Looking Across the Fields and Watching the Birds Fly,"

> . . . nature caught in a glass
> And there become a spirit's mannerism,
> A glass aswarm with things going as far as they can.

NOTES

1. W. B. Yeats, *The Collected Poems of W. B. Yeats* (New York: Macmillan, 1956), p. 232; hereafter cited as WBY.
2. Wallace Stevens, *The Collected Poems of Wallace Stevens* (New York: Knopf, 1954), p. 374; hereafter cited as CP.
3. Wallace Stevens, *Opus Posthumous*, ed. Samuel French Morse (New York: Knopf, 1957), pp. 116-17; hereafter cited as OP.

PART TWO

Other Modern Poets

Rain

The rain is alive with ancient symmetries.
It is a god of the air that on my head,
My shoulders, my hips and my feet
Blesses with care and refreshment,

Soul of my soul, ultimately unknowable,
The rain is alive as an animal
As I am alive as an animal, and we
Share reality and share mystery,

The mystery of duration and of time
That is timeless after we shall end,

The sense as infinite while we have being.
Then rain shall fall on others, enfolding them.

BONNIE COSTELLO

"'Polished Garlands' of Agreeing Difference": William Carlos Williams and Marianne Moore, an Exchange

Marianne Moore and William Carlos Williams are often classed together as poets, and there are many reasons why they should be. They both resided in New York and participated in the activities of the New York avant-garde, made up mostly of visual artists. They both developed a sense of the particular in their poetry, far beyond the tenets of imagism. Of all the moderns, they showed the greatest democracy of subject matter and diction and included the most found material. Beyond this, they are identified because they wrote about each other often and specifically because Williams repeatedly makes Moore the heroine of the modernist project to save the line from stodginess.[1] As he wrote in his autobiography: "like a rafter holding up the superstructure of our uncompleted building . . . she was our saint."[2]

Moore's response, made to Donald Hall some years later, showed her characteristic humility, but perhaps also a need to curtail Williams' efforts to identify her aspirations with his own: "I never was a rafter holding up anyone!"[3] When we trace the relationship of these two modernists, in their essays about one another, in their private correspondence, and in their poetry, we see a tremendous mutuality but also a growing rift over fundamental questions of style and decorum. These differences are important precisely because the challenges these poets made to conventional thought and expression have so much in common. Williams saw the radical core of Moore's art immediately and embraced it emphatically. Moore showed greater reserve toward Williams, respecting his energy but not his audacity. The many echoes of self-criticism in her poetry suggest that she may well have suspected Williams' radical spirit the more for recognizing herself in it. Certainly Williams, despite his impressionistic style, remains one of the best critics of Moore, and his remarks on her work apply well to his own, though with important differences. On the surface Williams seems the more radical of the two poets, but one might speculate from remarks in their prose and correspondence that a submerged pattern of motives existed beneath the expressed ones, in which Williams can be seen as the initially tamer mind, constantly struggling (with brilliant flashes of success) to let the lion out and Moore can be seen as the wilder, more effusive spirit constantly trying to harness itself into communicability and acceptability. Whatever the deep motives of their exchange, their relationship raises significant questions about the means and matter of modern poetry. Williams combined, at times even identified, the act of making forms with a rebellion against and de-creation of form in order to release the multiple impulses of the imagination and to make contact with the creative present. Moore was less iconoclastic but more idiosyncratic. For her, form provided a means of giving communal shape and decorum and thus permanence and transfiguring grace to the iridescent movements of the imagination in its creative preoccupation with the immediate. Thus they worked at cross-purposes, though often with similar results.

I

Moore and Williams discovered each other through *Others*, a magazine of verse edited by Alfred Kreymborg, who discovered them both. Their early correspondence, while typically reticent on Moore's part and typically hyperbolic on Williams', suggests the natural warmth and mutuality of two young poets keeping company on the fringe. Who else would listen or sympathize? In February 1917 Moore wrote to Williams in praise of his book *Al Que Quiere or The Pleasures of Democracy*: "Your compression makes one feel that the Japanese haven't the field to themselves." But she did not hesitate to add a remark from her mother (often the switch behind Moore's efforts of restraint): "people who read y[ou]r book w[ou]ld be more attracted by something bold."[4] Williams' letter in April was a ray of spring enthusiasm. He opens: "Marianne Moore—it is a pleasure to say that name."[5]

Kora in Hell, Williams' naked lunge against the mind's repressions, was published in 1920 and Robert McAlmon of *Contact* asked Moore to review it. Her comments, though generally applauding the work, mark the differences between her and Williams.[6] Williams is a poet, Moore writes, of "concise, energetic disgust . . . the acknowledgment of our debt to the imagination constitutes, perhaps, his positive value. Compression, colour, speed, accuracy and that restraint of instinctive craftsmanship which precludes anything dowdy or laboured."[7] Having duly admired his performance, however (and converting his principle of release into a principle of restraint), she takes him to task for some of his more reckless tendencies and remarks. She makes a point of dismissing those areas in which Williams identifies his poetic strength, replacing them with more classical poetic virtues:

> "By the brokenness of his composition," he writes, "the poet makes himself master of a certain weapon which he could possess himself in no other way." We do not so much feel the force of this statement as we feel that there is in life as there is in Sir Francis Bacon the ability to see resemblances in things which are dissimilar; in the ability to see such differences, a special kind of imagination is required which Dr. Williams has.

She turns away from his destructive and negative impulses and toward his ordering, unifying impulses. Williams, she hints throughout the essay, is good *despite* his foolish notions—intellectual, skillful, and sophisticated despite his "championing of the school of ignorance, or rather no school but experience." Her ambivalence toward Williams' aesthetic (and her sense that his strengths and weaknesses arise from the same impulses) is revealed in the very syntax characteristic of the essay: "If he rates audacity too high as an aesthetic asset, there can be no doubt that he has courage of the kind which is a necessity and not merely an admired accessory. . . . The sharpened faculties which require exactness, instant satisfaction and an underpinning of truth are too abrupt in their activities sometimes to follow; but the niceness and effect of vigour for which they are responsible are never absent."

Moore criticizes Williams most severely for challenging the most classical elements of poetry, rhetoric, and rhyme: " 'Nowadays poets spit upon rhyme and rhetoric,' he says. His work provides examples of every rhetorical principle insisted on by rhetoricians and one wonders upon what ground he has been able to persuade himself that poets spit upon rhyme?"

Williams' response, in a letter, is firm in defending his motives, if finally deferential in regretting results.

> Perhaps you are right in your adverse view of my sometimes obstreperous objections to decorum. I must think more of

that. But each must free himself from the bonds of banality as
best he can; you or another may turn into a lively field of
intelligent activity quite easily but I, being perhaps more
timid or unstable at heart, must free myself by more violent
methods. I cannot object to rhetoric, as you point out, but I
must object to the academic associations with which
rhetoric is hung and which vitiate all its significance by
making the piece of work to which it is applied a dried bone.
And so I have made the mistake of abusing the very thing I
most use. The same with rhyme: who can object to rhyme
except in the sense of the pendulum's swing against it
brought about by stupid usage? I thank you for calling my
attention to these inaccuracies.[8]

Despite her reservations about *Kora*, Williams made Moore the
resident saint of *Spring and All* (1923). And his remarks about her, while
impressionistic, were more astute than any others that appeared previously, revealing qualities she would perhaps have been less eager to
herald. Most significantly, he noticed that the energy of Moore's verse
flowed toward composition and design rather than toward representation and that her works resisted the attachments of association and
moved toward an autonomy and self-sufficiency. The important discovery Williams made in the prose of *Spring and All*, with Moore as his
test case, was that art is essentially formal, that subject matter or
content in the narrow sense (as distinguishable from "substance,"
which is always "the imagination") is the lure that engages consciousness in essentially formal processes of transformation. "The incompre-
hensibility of her poems is witness to at what cost (she cleaves herself
away) as it is also to the distance which most are from a comprehension
of the purpose of composition."[9]

In attempting to represent this new art that moves away from subject
matter and toward the source and substance of "imagination," Williams
has constant recourse to the primal image of "prismatic color," which
he borrows from Moore's poem "In the Days of Prismatic Color."
Williams employs the image to posit a state of pure poetry, but his
idealism distinguishes him from Moore, who sees this as a prelapsarian
condition only, as her title suggests. Williams articulates his appreciation of Moore's modernity more completely in his essay "Marianne
Moore" (1925). Using metaphors of geometry he observes that "it is a
multiplication of impulses that by their several flights, crossing at all
eccentric angles, might enlighten." The point of intersection, he notes,

is that area of "white penetration" in which imagination is substance. Developing points raised in *Spring and All* he cites Moore's rapidity and "lack of connectives" (rather than abstraction or distortion) as means of freeing words from their semantic and prosodic frames, rinsing them of thinking, "clean perfect, unnicked beside other words in parade." Though her means of achieving these results are different (more discreet) than Williams', there is considerable insight in his remarks. One suspects, however, that Moore might have felt a little uncomfortably exposed by such observations. In her own discussions of her art she insists on directness and plain speaking, on representational accuracy, on moral substance. The suggestions that she "cleaves herself" from her subject would certainly have jarred her, though it concurs with the experience of her difficult surfaces. Williams was right in seeing the simple rhetorical and thematic outlines of Moore's art as "recognizable edges against the ground which cannot, as she might desire, be left entirely white." Her art is essentially abstract and formal, for all her claims to make form expedient and meaning down-to-earth. And for all her claims to "naturalness" her work is, as Williams observed in praise of it, "a set-off porcelain garden."[10]

Williams won *The Dial* Award in 1926, while Moore was editor. The announcement of the award by Scofield Thayer and J. S. Watson noted that the *The Dial* Award "'crowns' no book" but is intended to supplement the income of an artist who "has done a service to letters." Moore asked Wallace Stevens to write the tribute, but he declined (protesting a heavy burden of family obligations) so Moore wrote a brief comment herself, quoting from Stevens' ambivalent reply: "'What Columbus discovered is nothing to what Williams is searching for.'" Moore's own remarks were respectful and descriptive. She observed Williams' physician's attention to objects, the disconnected and centrifugal quality of his forms, his opposition to "'falseness,'" and most of all his "courage."[11]

Williams' devotion to Moore continued through the twenties and thirties. In June of 1932 he wrote to her after seeing several of her new poems (which were written after a long hiatus during the *Dial* years and which would later appear in *Selected Poems*), and his language was more laudatory than ever. "There is no work in verse being done in any language which I can read which I find more to my liking and which I believe to be so thoroughly excellent." In particular he celebrates her use of the local. "The meaning of the objective, the realization of its releasing quality instead of its walling effect when badly comprehended has been nowhere so well forced to the light."[12] Indeed, during this period Moore began to extend her use of the particular, enriching the weave of her poems with the rich textures of descriptive and scientific detail for which she is known. And yet it is just such profusions, "such releasing qualities," that she often cut from later versions of her poems. Aesthetic and thematic integration must prevail. Although Williams lauds her sense of the objective, she seems ambivalent about his indiscriminate faith in it, perhaps privately echoing Stevens' remark that not all things are equal. While in a letter in 1934 she "bless[es] the collective wheel barrow," her essay on Williams that year, "Things Others Never Notice," is more discriminating: "The poem often is about nothing that we wish to give our attention to, but if it is something he wishes our attention for, what is urgent for him becomes urgent for us. His uncompromising conscientiousness sometimes seems misplaced; he is at times almost insultingly specific, but there is in him—and this must be our consolation—that dissatisfied expanding energy, the emotion, the *ergo* of the medieval dialectician, the 'therefore' which is the distinguishing mark of the artist."[13] That Moore should object to "uncompromising conscientiousness" and specificity is surprising when we think of poems like "An Octopus," "The Plumet Basilisk," "The Jerboa," and others. Moore shares his "dissatisfied expanding energy," which shows itself in her omnivorous lines. But as her own poems also show, she was highly suspicious of this energy. Her poetry records a constant tension between the desire to be neat, to conform to "correct writing," and the desire to include, which makes correct writing seem foolish, and this tension often finds its way into her responses to Williams. We think of her own verse (and of Williams' observations on it) when she writes: "Disliking the tawdriness of unnecessary explanation, the detracting compulsory connective, stock speech of any kind, he sets words down, 'each note secure in its own posture—singularly woven.' . . . Williams objects to urbanity—to sleek and natty effects—and this is a good sign if not always a good thing."[14]

Moore admired much in Williams' book *An Early Martyr* and told him so in a letter in October 1935: "You are doing here what you seem to think Gertrude Stein is doing, in making words live." Williams' essay on Stein observed that her goal was "to keep a beleaguered line of understanding which has movement from breaking down and becoming a hole into which we sink decoratively to rest."[15] Moore seems not to have identified herself with this procedure, but it may not be irrelevant to observe that Stevens, in a letter to Ronald Lane Latimer, remarked that Moore was achieving the same kind of originality as Stein, but with more substance.[16]

While Moore's letter begins enthusiastically, the reservations inevitably intrude. And this time the reservations deal with fundamental matters of propriety, the personal side of aesthetic decorum: "I could go on this way, of every one; *nearly* everyone; for there are some I shall never understand; nor why it is necessary you should do a certain thing. One's compulsions are tyrants; one suffers for them . . . I cannot see that art is in any way different from the rest of life, from conversation or from the strategies of solitude; and it is an unending query with me why a person would say on the page what he has never been known to say to your face." For Moore, writing was a way of taking imaginary possession of life through self-conscious artifice. Her attempt was to create such imaginary gardens while at the same time attending to the rich and various nuances of experience that baffle and enchant the mind as they thwart its will to order. In transforming experience into art, she strove for a rigorous decorum that could retain the dazzling inconsistency of things. In this she resembles Wallace Stevens, whose rhetorical and prosodic outlines frame dithering figurations. For Williams, art was release from the restrictions and repressions and exclusions of life. Moore and Williams found themselves at odds because her rage for order in the messiness of life was counter to his rage for chaos in the boundaries of culture. Williams' reply made no concessions:

> I thoroughly sympathize with your position. But to me a book is somewhat of a confessional. It is just because I do not say things-that-I-would-say that I must write them. It would not be fair to a reader for me to hold back knowledge of the matrix from which comes the possible gem.
>
> It goes further than that with me. There is a good deal of rebellion in what I write, rebellion against stereotype poetic process—the too meticulous choice among other things. In too much refinement there lurks a sterility that wishes to pass too often for purity when it is anything but that. Coarseness for its own sake is inexcusable but a Rabelaisian sanity requires that the rare and the fine be exhibited as coming like everything else from the dirt. There is no incompatibility between them.[17]

The letters between Moore and Williams fell off during the forties, and there was little discussion of aesthetics. The rift over decorum became permanent in 1951, when Barbara Asch of New Directions asked Moore for a quotation to advertise *Paterson IV*. She refused, replying that while she still admired Williams' virtuosity, she regretted his lack of self-restraint, especially in his treatment of sexuality. Book IV seemed, to her, to display more license than art. Williams' reply made no defense, but rather acknowledged differences, an act undoubtedly difficult because of his previous devotion to Moore. "It is inevitable that, in the end, individuals, brothers though they be and allied as they have lived will finally *arrive* at the place where their separate individualities are revealed and they find themselves strangers. That will be the moment when their love and their faith is most tested. Let it be so with us."[18] Moore, in return, saluted this gesture and made a concession, which has the mark of sincerity: "The fact is, I must admit, that we usually exemplify—in some measure—the faults against which we inveigh. I am prone to excess, in art as in life, so that I resist anything which implies that the line of least resistance is normal. . . . Is it after all, loyalty which makes one resistful?"

This place where separate individualities are revealed, and also this place of loyalty and similarity (where one exemplifies what one inveighs against), can be seen in the poems as much as the prose of these two writers. There are many directions from which this place might be approached, but if we consider early debates between Williams and Moore over the decorum of rhetoric and prosody, in relation to some early poems, we can see how the poems express deep-rooted tensions.

II

Since Williams' *Spring and All* so persistently invokes Moore as the *miglior fabbro*, it is appropriate to compare a poem from that book with one of Moore's poems. And since they both wrote poems employing the classic image of the rose, our subject for comparison is given.

Williams' well-known poem, later entitled "The Rose," is part of a polemic against a representational theory of linguistic meaning. He will not tolerate, he insists, either the "plagiarism of nature"—mimetic description—or "crude symbolism"—the use of natural objects as signs for emotional states or ideas. In place of these Williams exalts "design" as an autonomous function of the imagination. He runs into a problem, however, in attempting this conversion, since it is the representational function of language that his audience knows and expects. This problem was responsible for the sometimes insurmountable difficulty of *Kora in Hell*. His solution is to provide "the forms common to experience" (both images and rhetorical structures) "so as not to frighten the onlooker away but to invite him" but "at the same time to detach them from ordinary experience to the imagination." Between these prose remarks Williams sets "The Rose" to illustrate how words and images may be cut loose from their representational functions and freed in the field of the imagination. This idea of broken assertion charges all the poems of *Spring and All* on the theory that it is "so easy to slip into the old mold, so hard to cling firmly to the advance" that thought, continually lapsing into ritualized forms and repressions, must be disrupted and renewed in flashes of inspiration. The opening of "The Rose" provides just such a disruption of ritual, wiping away with one gesture a whole history of associations.

> The rose is obsolete
> but each petal ends in
> an edge, the double facet
> cementing the grooved
> columns of air—the edge
> cuts without cutting
> meets—nothing—renews
> itself in metal or porcelain—
>
> whither? It ends—
>
> But if it ends
> the start is begun
> so that to engage roses
> becomes a geometry—
>
> Sharper, neater, more cutting
> figured in majolica—
> the broken plate
> glazed with a rose
>
> Somewhere the sense
> makes copper roses
> steel roses—
>
> The rose carried weight of love
> but love is at an end—of roses
> It is at the edge of the
> petal that love waits
>
> Crisp, worked to defeat
> laboredness—fragile
> plucked, moist, half-raised
> cold, precise, touching

What

The place between the petal's
edge and the

From the petal's edge a line starts
that being of steel
infinitely fine, infinitely
rigid penetrates
the Milky Way
without contact—lifting
from it—neither hanging
nor pushing—

The fragility of the flower
unbruised
penetrates space.[19]

If the concept of love continues to play a role in the poem in connection with the rose, it is as something hard-edged, independent and particular, not the traditional soft blur. Feelings, like things, are known by their edges. Both become infinite when those edges are removed from limiting contexts. Both symbolic and sensory associations are contradicted by the incongruous ideas and qualities of geometry and metal. Conventional unities of voice, setting, temporal sequence, grammar and rhetoric, punctuation, prosody, even subject matter, are all similarly disrupted in the attempt to reopen the ordering experience. The expectation of logical or sequential development is met with constant renewals, not just conceptually but at every level of organization. Syntactic connections are broken, leaving quick, suspended words and phrases. The dash replaces forms of punctuation with more closural force and indicates a struggle to imagine for which no single reference can be found, but in which thought collides with thought in breathless succession. The intersecting non sequiturs might indeed be called geometric in the sense Williams used the word to describe Moore's poems, "from all angles lines converging and crossing establish points." And yet they leave an impression of crisis, collision, and incompleteness, of old unities destroyed in preparation for a new unity of the imagination, not yet established but toward which sounds, rhythms, and images conspire.

Like Williams' "The Rose," Moore's poem "Roses Only" is an attempt to refute the old pieties of the rose by a principle of recalcitrance. And like Williams, Moore strives for perspective by incongruity. But she preserves the decorum of statement even while she constructs a "detached" imaginative design. And rather than exploding rhetoric and symbolism she stretches and redirects them to her advantage, giving an appearance of decorum and propriety to her subversive, independent act of mind. The poem makes bold use of personification, sequential logic, syntactic balance, and subordination. But such structural and figurative devices conduct readers through a gyroscopic dance of thought and feeling in which at each stop we are left reeling. By working a rhetorical clarity against a conceptual ambiguity, Moore, like Williams, loosens words from their various jostlings and teases the reader away from habitual responses to discover the dynamic play of word against word and phrase against phrase within an overall design.

Jean Garrigue has called "Roses Only" "a model of ambiguity" in which "a virtue is made of writing on two subjects as if they were one."[20] It works the other way around as well; Moore writes on one subject as if they were two and presents a unified but complex (ambivalent) attitude toward it. This poem combines criticism and praise, the same phenomena approached by volleying different points of view and, at each ironic turn, redefining the terms of evaluation.

> You do not seem to realize that beauty is a liability rather
> than an asset—that in view of the fact that spirit
>   creates form we are justified in supposing
>   that you must have brains. For you, a symbol of the
>   unit, stiff and sharp,
>   conscious of surpassing by dint of native superiority and
>   liking for everything
> self-dependent, anything an

> ambitious civilization might produce: for you unaided, to
>   attempt through sheer
>   reserve, to confuse presumptions resulting from
>   observation, is idle. You cannot make us
>   think you a delightful happen-so. But rose, if you are
>   brilliant, it
>   is not because your petals are the without-which-nothing
>   of pre-eminence. Would you not, minus

thorns, be a what-is-this, a mere

> peculiarity? They are not proof against a worm, the
>   elements, or mildew;
>   but what about the predatory hand? What is brilliance
>   without co-ordination? Guarding the
>   infinitesimal pieces of your mind, compelling audience
>   to
>   the remark that it is better to be forgotten than to be
>   remembered too violently,
> your thorns are the best part of you.[21]

Moore has managed to write a poem that admits the full complexity of feeling without sacrificing surface coherence. She works by retort rather than confrontation. It is a feminist poem, countering Edmund Waller's advice in "Go, Lovely Rose" by arguing the liability of beauty. Rose cannot escape attention, her modesty alone failing to ward off an audience determined to exalt and possess her. Only by a harshness can she stay the predatory hand that might destroy her self-dependence. Though Waller may warn that beauty dies, Rose has more immediate worries. However, Moore's message is not directed to men, but to the rose, who has become dangerously fond of her supposed advantage as a thing admired. Her strength is not in modesty, then, but in standoffishness and cruelty. Her perfection resides in what would seem to mar perfection. An ideal beauty is not superior but self-protective.

Garrigue does not name the two subjects, but she is presumably referring to the major inversion of the poem, in which the admiration is transferred from the intrinsic virtues of the rose (beauty, intelligence) to its inadvertent value as a moral example. Again Moore's irony is built on a disparity and inversion of perspectives. But she does not rest on a single opposition between the rose's sense of how she is perceived and her audience's sense of her value. The language takes another turn, for the perspectives of both rose and audience are themselves complex. In the first turn, the rose's deep brilliance, of which she herself is confident, is perceived in spite of her efforts to appear as "a delightful happen-so": in the second turn, the speaker surpasses the public point of view, identifying the rose's real worth not as she herself imagines it, in her "native superiority," but in the alienating effects of that superiority that prevent admiration from becoming envy.

At the level of the metaphor, Moore's irony takes similar turns, through which she again both accepts and reinvents conventional symbolism. While her admiration transfers from the rose to the thorns, the logic of the metaphor has already shifted to refute simple oppositions, so that the rose and its thorns become identified. The rose is even a symbol of its thorns, its self-conscious superiority, its unattainability. Similarly "brilliance" is reassigned, not only from physical to intellectual categories but also to moral ones. The ultimate wit of the poem rests in its tonal ambiguity. Typically, Moore goes beyond obvious forms of vanity to detect and debunk subtle ones, like the pose of humility when it disguises egotism. Finding brilliance that pretends a casualness about itself that it does not in fact feel, Moore retorts by acknowledging and then dismissing that brilliance, preferring the true lesson of humility it teaches to the common world beneath it. Moore defeats her subject—exposing vanity disguised as humility—only, ironically, to raise it again on a new pedestal. Moore challenges traditional symbolism, then, by deeply complicating and revising the terms of association, but also by so overwhelming the image with the argument that she no longer makes any imposition on nature but declares her own artifice just as Williams did by different means.

But while we are hunting out these turns of meaning, our imagination is engaged in a number of other ways. We become less concerned with the statement being made than with the formal compositional elegance of the rhetoric itself, the rhythm of simple sentences against complex ones, the tension in the suspended predicates, the epigrammatic swiftness of the conclusion. Moore plays her meanings off against the elegance of these devices, making conceptual and figurative leaps that require a different pace of apprehension. The rhetoric, that is, causes us to take in much more than we can fully accommodate logically, with the result that phrases and words spin off centrifugally from their frames and affect us alogically. Moore's prosody pulls the reader according to yet another ordering motion. While Williams uses the rhythm of jagged thought, Moore subjects her words to the discipline of syllabic count and rhyme, creating a counterpoint of aural and visual structures. But rather than supporting other organizational principles in the poem, the count and the rhyme work independently. The result is that words are very much jostled in the poem, but according to so many disparate orders that words indeed tremble in their settings, shaking off the barnacles of thought. Coming at their materials from different points of departure, these two poets have similar, though distinguishable, results in creating a theater for the reader's own imaginative action.

Like Williams, Moore knew the dangers of rhetoric, but rather than shattering or occluding it she discovered ways to turn it to her advantage. When all the elements of a poem move in one direction the rhetoric is invisible and delusive. But recognized as artifice, it can have the power of sponsoring, rather than repressing, a rich and multiple act of imagination. With this awareness Moore could achieve the appearance of impeccable correctness she wanted without compromising the more effusive impulses of her mind. Williams, then, held rhetoric and formal decorum as his chief obstacle, to be blasted, penetrated, transcended in an effort to reach the "white penetration" of imagination and reality. Moore held rhetoric and formal decorum as valuable tools in creating her compositions, in lending harmony and equilibrium to the restless movements of consciousness.

In "Those Various Scalpels" Moore uses such strategies even more boldly and effectively than in "Roses Only." Here she indeed proves Williams' point about her, in using "the same material as others before her" but coming "at it effectively at a new angle." She has chosen one of the most classical of rhetorical forms—the blazon of beauties, in which a woman's physical attributes are compared to various precious objects. But Moore takes this form in unexpected directions, making astonishing figurative leaps, compounding metaphor with metaphor, and entering each comparison with such detail that the object at hand is momentarily forgotten in the richness of analogy. Thus the particular is given full attention without negating the act of comparison.

THOSE VARIOUS SCALPELS,

those
various sounds consistently indistinct, like intermingled
echoes struck from thin glasses successively at random—
the inflection disguised: your hair, the tails of two
fighting-cocks head to head in stone like sculptured
scimitars repeating the curve of your ears in reverse
order: your eyes,
flowers of ice and snow

sown by tearing winds on the cordage of disabled ships; your
raised hand,

an ambiguous signature: your cheeks, those rosettes
 of blood on the stone floors of French châteaux,
with regard to which the guides are so affirmative—your
 other hand,

a bundle of lances all alike, partly hid by emeralds from
 Persia and the fractional magnificence of Florentine
 goldwork—a collection of little objects—
sapphires set with emeralds, and pearls with a moonstone,
 made fine
 with enamel in gray, yellow, and dragonfly blue; a
 lemon, a pear

and three bunches of grapes, tied with silver: your dress, a
 magnificent square
 cathedral tower of uniform
 and at the same time diverse appearance—a
species of vertical vineyard rustling in the storm
 of conventional opinion. Are they weapons or
 scalpels?
 Whetted to brilliance

by the hard majesty of that sophistication which is superior
 to opportunity,
 these things are rich instruments with which to
 experiment.
 But why dissect destiny with instruments
 more highly specialized than components of destiny
 itself?[22]

This witty tour de force portrays a lady of excessive sophistication, of elegance without genuine grace, suggesting that her self-conscious, overrefined appearance works against her. She has tried to take too much control of her destiny and consequently she has lost touch with nature. The poem also, perhaps, mocks the kind of baroque poetry that might interest such a lady, in line with Shakespeare's "My Mistress' Eyes." The poem may even be a self-directed warning not to lose sight of the natural, as this lady has done.

Moore's poem is itself highly artificial and almost baroque, but she counters its imposing symmetries in a number of ways. While the rhetoric assures readers a sense of direction, we are permitted many delightful side trips, which become the most valuable part of the journey. Williams is insightful in seeing Moore's simplicity of design as a way of giving black outline to her prismatic thought. When we are reading we lose track of the design, but it is there, as in Henry James' oriental carpet, when we step back. We are reminded of the compositional outline when we reach the end of the poem, but the figure of the lady hardly holds up as a specific reference under this wonderful overload of comparison. Thus a rhetorical neatness of the closure sets off a semantic richness. The formal structure of the stanzas and the simple, unaccented rhymes work with the rhetorical outlines to present this density of thought and imagery.

Williams wrote a poem, called "Portrait of a Lady," also using this form, but his response was to throw comparison aside for the sake of the particular. The high rhetorical voice that would import natural objects for their emotional and conceptual value is repeatedly interrupted by a voice preoccupied with things, whose interest pulls away from the primary subject toward each object to which it is compared. The result is a deliberate portrait of confusion, of rhetoric unraveled by the pull of the particular.

> Your thighs are appletrees
> whose blossoms touch the sky.
> Which sky? The sky
> where Watteau hung a lady's
> slipper. Your knees
> are a southern breeze—or
> a gust of snow. Agh! what
> sort of man was Fragonard?
> — as if that answered
> anything. Ah, yes—below
> the knees, since the tune
> drops that way, it is
> one of those white summer days,
> the tall grass of your ankles
> flickers upon the shore —
> Which shore? —
> the sand clings to my lips —
> Which shore?
> Agh, petals maybe. How
> should I know?
> Which shore? Which shore?
> I said petals from an appletree.[23]

Moore too allowed her imagination to stray in this way, straining the format and inverting the hierarchy of analogy, but she was always eventually drawn back to the primary subject and to the rhetorical outline, whereas Williams abandoned these entirely, leaving the impression of bewildering, if charming, incompleteness.

If we compare the early careers of Williams and Moore, the heroine of *Spring and All* appears the more accomplished poet. Williams wrote many brilliant poems during the twenties that are still a thrill to encounter, but part of their thrill is their rawness, their courage. They express a primitive struggle to wring the neck of rhetoric, to dismantle the old order and herald a new beginning. They are experimental flashes rather than completed visions. Moore's early work has the mark of a virtuoso, combining the power of formal eloquence and precision with an exhilarating alertness to the flux of feeling and observation. She managed in her early work to maintain a dynamic equilibrium between propriety and recalcitrance, between the will to be understood and the sense of elusive beauty and particularity, between the grace of rhetoric and the dazzle of deviation.

But Williams' work after the mid-thirties seems far more powerful and permanent than Moore's work of the same period. Williams began to discover a kind of order in art (which he named "measure") that would not become repressive but would, instead, release the mind into graceful action. Williams continued to struggle against ritualized ideas and forms, but such combat had become a positive structure in his thought, a ritual against ritual. Moore, too, was successful in terms of the priorities she had evolved of communicability and propriety but less successful poetically since such priorities can damage art when they outweigh absorption and recalcitrance. Her late poems too comfortably embrace their household truths and charms. There is little tension between poet and audience and thus little challenge. In her rage for order she eventually lost her natural will to digress, so that her consistent inconsistency became the dogmatic theme rather than the enchanting structure of her art.

NOTES

1. *The Autobiography of William Carlos Williams* (New York: Random House, 1948), p. 148.
2. *Autobiography*, p. 146.
3. *A Marianne Moore Reader* (New York: Viking, 1961), p. 257.

4. The letters of Marianne Moore are unpublished. They are housed at the Museum of the Philip H. and A. S. W. Rosenbach Foundation in Philadelphia. I am grateful to Clive E. Driver, Director of the Foundation and Literary Executor of the Estate of Marianne C. Moore, for permission to quote from them. Copyright on all unpublished material belongs to the Moore Estate; it cannot be quoted without permission of Clive E. Driver.

5. From an unpublished letter. I am grateful to James Laughlin for permission to quote from this letter.

6. They also echo in several ways comments Wallace Stevens had made on *Al Que Quiere* (comments that Williams boldly included in his prologue to *Kora*) and indicate the beginnings of significant sympathy between Moore and Stevens. A few years later Moore wrote the most positive of all reviews of *Harmonium*. Moore's poetry is very close to Stevens' in its rage for order, its iridescent textures of imagery against simple outlines of rhetoric and prosody, and its essential abstraction.

7. All quotations from Moore's review are from *Contact*, No. 4 (Summer 1921), pp. 5–8.

8. *The Selected Letters of William Carlos Williams*, ed. John C. Thirwall (New York: McDowell, Obolensky, 1957), p. 52.

9. *Spring and All* (1923) rpt. in *Imaginations* (New York: New Directions, 1970), p. 101.

10. All quotations in this paragraph are from "Marianne Moore" (1931), *Selected Essays of William Carlos Williams* (New York: Random House, 1954), pp. 121–31.

11. *Predilections* (New York: Viking, 1955), pp. 134–36.

12. *Selected Letters*, pp. 122–23.

13. *Predilections*, pp. 136–39.

14. *Predilections*, p. 137.

15. *Selected Essays*, p. 118.

16. *Letters of Wallace Stevens*, ed. Holly Stevens (New York: Knopf, 1966), p. 290.

17. *Selected Letters*, pp. 155–56.

18. *Selected Letters*, pp. 303–04.

19. *Spring and All*, pp. 107–10.

20. Jean Garrigue, *Marianne Moore* (Minneapolis: Univ. of Minnesota Press, 1955), p. 9.

21. Marianne Moore, *Selected Poems* (New York: Macmillan, 1935), p. 421.

22. *The Complete Poems of Marianne Moore* (New York: Macmillan/Viking, 1967), pp. 51–52.

23. Wallace Stevens, *The Collected Earlier Poems* (New York: New Directions, 1951), p. 40.

JOHN F. SEARS

The Subversive Performer
in Frost's
"Snow" and "Out, Out—"

Frost first published the poems "Snow" and "Out, Out—" in 1916, when he was just beginning to reach a popular audience.[1] Although it may not be apparent at first glance, the two poems display similar dramatic qualities, and I believe Frost recognized this when he placed them fairly close together toward the end of his third book, *Mountain Interval*. They appear among a group of poems that in varied ways reflect a streak of wildness—sometimes comic, sometimes eerie or bearish—in Frost's imagination: "Out, Out —," "Brown's Descent," "The Gum-Gatherer," "The Line-Gang," "The Vanishing Red," "Snow," "The Sound of Trees."

In the case of "Snow," it is significant that the poem appeared toward the end of Frost's first year of "barding around," since it is so much concerned with talk as a means of holding and teasing an audience. Meserve, the protagonist, comes closest of any of Frost's characters to Frost's own public persona, to the man who enjoyed playing with an audience, even "putting them on" a bit. He also embodies the less admirable aspects of that personality: evasiveness, coyness, lack of appreciation for the sympathy of others. But Meserve most resembles Frost—both the platform performer and the persona in the poems—in the subversive quality of his imagination. Meserve's capacity for sly talk relates him not only to the mischievous farmer poet of "Mending Wall" but also to the speakers of poems like "Out, Out—." Although the poet of "Out, Out —" could hardly be called comic, the strategies he adopts in telling his tale are similar to the ones Meserve employs. In this kind of poem, Frost, like Meserve, is interested in lighting up that mysterious borderline between fact and fancy where our practical hold on reality begins to break down. In playful, sometimes nightmarish ways he challenges our comfortable assumptions.

I

Meserve is a version of the persona Frost was trying out on the platform and in smaller groups during the years 1913 to 1916. Frost must have been frequently concerned with the way he presented himself in talk in those years. For the first time, he was sharing his work and his ideas about poetry with his fellow poets and, after returning from England, beginning to court a popular audience. But if Frost portrays some aspects of his increasingly successful persona in Meserve, he also parodies that self. Meserve is a run-on talker; he shares Frost's need to dominate the conversation, a need that was already established in Frost the private performer before he mastered the public role. In his poem "The Golden Room," Wilfred Gibson remembers an evening in England in 1914 when Frost held forth to a group of the Georgian poets:

> In the lamplight
> We talked and laughed; but, for the most part, listened
> While Robert Frost kept on and on and on,
> In his slow New England fashion, for our delight,
> Holding us with shrewd turns and racy quips,
> And the rare twinkle of his grave blue eyes.[2]

Frost's first performances before larger, less intimate audiences were not always successful. He was paralyzed by fear, he read badly, and he felt too constrained to let himself go in talk.[3] But as he became more confident he used his wit and evasive playfulness to create a self-protective distance between himself and his audience. According to his close friend Theodore Morrison, Frost "used light and not-so-light words to tease and flout, both privately and on the platform, and made himself a place apart behind their shelter."[4] In "Snow" Frost dramatizes this subversive style by engaging Meserve in a form of contest with the couple in the poem.

The immediate source of conflict in the poem is Meserve's insistence on continuing his journey through a blizzard to his own farm, even though he has spent three hours traveling the first four miles. At least that is the issue for Fred and Helen Cole, who own the farm where

Meserve has stopped to rest his horses. The couple interpret the storm as a challenge to Meserve's physical stamina. Fred Cole is drawn to this challenge; Helen Cole thinks that only the foolish male ego could respond to it. Critics, too, have focused on Meserve's daring of the storm and, as a result, have made his journey into a fatuous "male quest." Marion Montgomery asserts that the "challenge" Meserve finds in the storm is part of the "war between man and the natural world." Meserve "must go and conquer the blizzard."[5] And Eban Bass regards Meserve with equal seriousness: "Meserve should be free to prove himself against the snow, which is nature sought out as an enemy."[6] It is true that when Helen Cole asks him why he must go on when no one wants him to, Meserve replies, " 'Well, there's—the storm. That says I must go on. / That wants me as a war might if it came. / Ask any man.' " But Frost immediately adds, "He threw that as something / To last her till he got outside the door." What seems to be a direct answer is only a temporary maneuver.

Like Frost himself, Meserve never explains. When talking with some students at Bread Loaf about "A Masque of Reason" and "A Masque of Mercy," Frost was asked, "What do *you* really believe?" "Oh, don't ask me that," he replied, "I go around the edges of it."[7] Meserve disregards the practical concerns of his hosts in order to pursue a long rambling discourse around the borders of their predicament. Knowing perfectly well that the Coles are troubled by his decision to press on but also curious to see how he will make out, he sets out to aggravate their ambivalent state of mind. When Helen Cole asks him, " 'what *did* your wife say on the telephone?' " Meserve points to the leaf of an open book lying on the table:

> "It moved
> Just then, I thought. It's stood erect like that,
> There on the table, ever since I came,
> Trying to turn itself backward or forward,
> I've had my eye on it to make out which:
> If forward, then it's with a friend's impatience —
> You see I know—to get you on to things
> It wants to see how you will take; if backward,
> It's from regret for something you have passed
> And failed to see the good of."
> (FR, p. 147)

Sensing that his indirection increases their impatience, he jokes about their uneasiness. The warmth and quiet of the living room give the

Coles' dog, lamp, and book leaf " 'their repose,' " he says, " 'Though for all anyone can tell, repose / May be the thing you haven't, yet you give it.' " Such teasing creates the distance that Frost established with his own audience, and in "Snow" that distance is comically underscored by the two kinds of discourse that run side by side: the pragmatic comments and questions of the Coles about the advisability of Meserve continuing his journey and Meserve's imaginative talk. Frost dramatizes this gap between Meserve and the Coles in various ways.

To Helen Cole, Meserve is an aberrant personality. She finds something grotesque in his " 'wretched little Racker Sect,' " his " 'ten children under ten years old,' " and his size (" 'the runt,' " she calls him). Like the stranger burdened with care in "Love and a Question" and the man out walking in the darkness in "The Fear," Meserve is one of the intruders who frighten Frost's couples. He embodies the strange, the threatening, and the unknown, as Frost suggests by establishing an eerie affinity between Meserve and his snowy adversary without: "He pointed with his hand from where it lay / Like a white crumpled spider on his knee." But he stands out from the other intruders in Frost's poetry by grasping his position as a dramatic opportunity and making the most of it. He begins by sharpening the contrast between the quiet and security of the Coles' living room and the inhospitableness of the storm without:

> "That leaf!
> It can't turn either way. It needs the wind's help.
> But the wind didn't move it if it moved.
> It moved itself. The wind's at naught in here.
> It couldn't stir so sensitively poised
> A thing as that. It couldn't reach the lamp
> To get a puff of black smoke from the flame,
> Or blow a rumple in the collie's coat.
> You make a little foursquare block of air,
> Quiet and light and warm, in spite of all
> The illimitable dark and cold and storm. . . ."
>
> (RF, p. 148)

He appreciates the warm safety of the Coles' living room, but by his presence and his "nightmare talk" he tests the line they draw so distinctly between the storm and themselves, just as the speaker of "Mending Wall" tries to unsettle the assumptions of his commonsense neighbor with talk of the "something" in nature that doesn't love a wall:

> "It looks as if
> Some pallid thing had squashed its features flat
> And its eyes shut with overeagerness
> to see what people found so interesting
> In one another, and had gone to sleep
> Of its own stupid lack of understanding,
> Or broken its white neck of mushroom stuff
> Short off, and died against the windowpane."
>
> (RF, pp. 148-49)

Meserve occupies the characteristic Frostian vantage point between the human world (usually represented by a house, a home, a marriage) and the natural world and, like the poet of "Tree at My Window," he finds a counterpart to his own restlessness in the turmoil of the storm. In playing back and forth across the borderline between inner and outer weather, Meserve breaks down the hermetic security of the Coles' "foursquare block of air" and allies himself with the energy of the storm. He discovers in the animated edge of a drift a counterweight to the motionless leaf of the book, and he announces his pleasure in this detail with the glee of a witch:

> "There where
> There is a sort of tunnel in the frost —
> More like a tunnel than a hole—way down
> At the far end of it you see a stir
> And quiver like the frayed edge of the drift
> Blown in the wind. I *like* that— I like *that*."
>
> (RF, pp. 149-50)

As a preacher Meserve presumably has strong religious beliefs that might sustain him during his struggle with the storm, but he keeps them hidden. Frost, says Reginald Cook, "was a hard man to pin down" when it came to the question of his religious beliefs,[8] and so is Meserve. Meserve's considerable religious potentialities, like Frost's, are expressed not in conventional theological references but in his nearly superstitious sensitivity to objects and forces in the outer world ("Nothing very religious can be done for people lacking in superstition," Frost says in his essay on Emerson).[9] He has a remarkable ability to make objects come tautly alive—" 'That leaf there in your open book! It moved / Just then' "—and to make emptiness palpable—" 'You can just see [the snow] glancing off the roof,' " he says, " 'Making a great scroll upward toward the sky, / Long enough for recording all our names on.' "

Meserve's unsettling imagination, which fascinates his hosts, resembles the cosmic mischievousness we find in poems like "Design" and "Desert Places," as well as in "Mending Wall," and the Coles in fact recognize Meserve's " 'gift / Of words' " as the gift of poetry: " 'Was ever such a man for seeing likeness?' " Meserve himself describes their dialogue as " 'playing our fancy,' " although he is the only one relaxed enough to do so. While the Coles are occupied with the commonsense problem before them, he makes poetry out of the details he notices. We are reminded again of the descriptions of Frost's manner on the platform: "he would charm packed audiences," Louis Untermeyer says, "not only with poems his listeners knew by heart but also with roaming commentaries, lightly profound and seriously playful, full of unexpected twists of thought, a verbal legerdemain which he manipulated with the skill and glee of a virtuoso actor who enjoyed acting."[10]

Meserve's powers as an artist are such that the senses of his hosts remain acutely heightened after he has left, while they wait anxiously to find out if he has reached home safely. Helen Cole "hears" the space in Meserve's house over the open telephone line: " 'I hear an empty room—you know—it sounds that way.' " And Fred teases his wife and pays a kind of mocking tribute to Meserve, by adopting Meserve's outlandish style: " 'You can't hear whether she has left the door / Wide open and the wind's blown out the lamp / And the fire's died and the room's dark and cold?' "

In the end, the Coles recognize with a mixture of frustration and admiration that what to them was a matter of worry was to Meserve "just his fun." The play of his own mind delights him. The storm and the Coles' concern for him provide the necessary stimulus to his imagination. Although such playfulness has its compulsive, even perverse, side, the Coles can't help being affected by Meserve's talk: " 'If that's the way he preaches! . . . The least thing set him going.' "

II

Meserve's power to make "the least thing" vibrate with an indeterminate, alarming expressiveness is the same power that Frost exercises in "Design" and "Desert Places" and also in "An Old Man's Winter Night," "The Bonfire," "The Fear," "The Hill Wife," and the two witch poems. In "Out, Out—" he uses it to make a lurid accident into something more subtle. Although one hesitates to call "Out, Out—" playful, Frost manipulates the details of setting and action with the tense excitement of someone telling a ghost story. Like Meserve, the poet matches his penchant for picking out each small fact with an equally strong tendency to undermine our ordinary manner of taking those facts.

"Out, Out—" is at least as dramatic as Frost's dialogues and monologues, and nature serves here, as in those poems, as the background against which the human drama is acted out. Frost sets the stage for the tragedy about to ensue by creating discord, both in the images and in the tone, between the calmness of nature at the close of day and the noise of the saw in the yard:

> The buzz saw snarled and rattled in the yard
> And made dust and dropped stove-length sticks of wood,
> Sweet-scented stuff when the breeze drew across it.
> And from there those that lifted eyes could count
> Five mountain ranges one behind the other
> Under the sunset far into Vermont.
> And the saw snarled and rattled, snarled and rattled,
> As it ran light, or had to bear a load.
> And nothing happened: day was all but done.
>
> (RF, p. 136)

Just at this point, and before the violent action begins, the shift in Frost's dramatic tone is most striking. Although the subversive performer works quietly here, rather than aggressively like Meserve, our appreciation of the poem depends on our sensitivity to his tactics. As we move from "day was all but done" to the next line, the tone lightens and becomes for a moment personal; the poet steps into the poem and talks sympathetically about the boy's plight:

> Call it a day, I wish they might have said
> To please the boy by giving him the half hour
> That a boy counts so much when saved from work.
>
> (RF, p. 136)

Nothing could be more carefully designed to scare us than the way this intimate voice speaks once and then withdraws. Even this is a form of teasing, although of the grimmest sort. By the end of the poem the poet has assumed the stoical, seemingly callous detachment of the boy's family: "No more to build on there. And they, since they / Were not the one dead, turned to their affairs."

The critics of "Out, Out—" have located much of the horror of the poem in the boy's terrifying moment of insight after the saw cuts his hand and have found his response understandable in sociological terms: "Then the boy saw all— / Since he was old enough to know, big boy /Doing a man's work, though a child at heart— / He saw all spoiled." According to John F. Lynen, the boy recognizes that the loss of his hand means the loss of the "instrument" of "power and creativity" in the adult world. In a society where survival depends on hard, manual work he has "lost the possibility of ever becoming fully a man."[11] This is indeed a reasonable explanation, but in uncovering a rational motive for the boy's behavior it reverses the process of the poem. The poet intends to disquiet our rationality, to put us in doubt. This strategy and its success are most apparent at the moment of the accident itself:

> His sister stood beside them in her apron
> To tell them "Supper." At the word, the saw,
> *As if* to prove saws knew what supper meant,
> Leaped out at the boy's hand, *or seemed* to leap—
> *He must have* given the hand. *However it was,*
> Neither refused the meeting.
> (RF, p. 136; italics mine)

Frost gives us this event from several angles at once, all of them frightening. First he suggests that the saw is, in our terms, bewitched —it is possessed of an animal-like appetite and will of its own. It leaps out at the boy's hand, or it looks as if it does, which is alarming enough. But these alternatives merely set us up, as do the questions in the last stanza of "Design," for something more horrifying. Being people of common sense we will tend to reject the notion that saws have appetites or can leap, just as we will tend to reject the idea in "Design" that moth, flower, and spider were brought together by some malevolent being. But in "Out, Out—" the unnerving alternative is not mere accident, the absence of design, but the possibility of some self-destructive impulse in the boy. If motive and will were involved, they had to come from him. "He must have *given* the hand": That line is dark with implication. It is as if the boy were possessed by some unconscious drive that compels him to sacrifice his hand to the saw.

Frost's technique of injecting psychological tension into things and events is strikingly apparent in the difference between "Out, Out—" and the newspaper description of the same accident. There is no reason to suppose that Frost read this account. He had become acquainted with the boy involved during summer visits to Franconia, and he learned of his death from the Lynches, the people with whom the Frost family boarded. But the newpaper version of the incident is just the kind of logical account of the accident that Frost would have heard:

> Raymond Tracy Fitzgerald . . . died at his home Thursday afternoon, March 24, as the result of an accident by which one of his hands was badly hurt in a sawing machine. The young man was assisting in sawing up some wood in his own dooryard with a sawing machine and accidentally hit the loose pulley, causing the saw to descend upon his hand, cutting and lacerating it badly. Raymond was taken into the house and a physician was immediately summoned, but he died very suddenly from the effects of the shock, which produced heart failure. . . .[12]

The writer explains the event logically and straightforwardly. He focuses first on the wholly inadvertent movement of the hand in hitting the pulley, then on the chain of cause-and-effect occurrences that this initial accident sets off: The hand moves the pulley, the pulley brings the saw down on the hand, the saw cuts the hand, the shock of being cut causes heart failure. There is nothing mysterious here, nothing that requires more than the simplest sort of scientific reasoning.

Much of the potential horror of the incident is lost because of the writer's assumption that there is nothing that cannot be accounted for in a matter-of-fact way. The world is a rational and orderly place. He sees the event entirely from the outside. As far as he is concerned the boy has no inner life that contributes in any way to his fate. Frost, on the other hand, opens up some dreadful psychological dimensions in the situation. In the poem we hear nothing about the hand hitting the pulley or the pulley drawing the saw down on the hand. Instead we hear that the saw "Leaped out at the boy's hand, or seemed to leap—," a totally unscientific and imaginative account, but possibly a more accurate one since it may capture the way the accident actually appeared. Frost then reaches beyond appearance into the boy's possible role in the event: "He must have *given* the hand." We also hear nothing of heart failure due to shock (at least not in the medical meaning of that term). Instead we hear that the boy "saw all spoiled." The shock is not physical, but psychological. We are left in doubt as to what "all" might encompass, but we know that for the boy his loss is total. Such a response remains extreme, whether or not it can be justified on rational grounds. The boy feels immediately, irrevocably shut out of life. That, Frost implies, is why he dies.

The force of "Out, Out —" comes finally not from the boy's hand being chopped off or from his abrupt death (disturbing enough in themselves), but from the way Frost effectively turns our attention toward the boy's inner life: his possible complicity in his fate and his certain recognition of its implications. After reading the poem we have the feeling that we have been visited, like the Coles, by a master of the uncanny who cannot be pinned down to an explanation of the events he has described or even to his own responses to those events and who thus undermines the familiar ground on which we stand.

"The fascination of a Frost performance," John Meixner says, "was the vibrant way he wove things together, how he continuously turned significance up out of the actual, the immediate occasion."[13] The "least thing" set him going. This, fortunately for us, is as true of the actor in the poems as it was of the performer on the platform. In "Out, Out —" we can see Frost's power at work in the way he transforms the bare facts of a boy's death. Perhaps Frost had the technique of *Macbeth* in mind as well as Macbeth's vision of the horror of life when he named the poem "Out, Out —." "*Macbeth*," he once said, "is a two-for-a-cent story but Shakespeare made it have all kinds of meaning."[14]

NOTES

1. "Out, Out—" first appeared in *McClure's*, July 1916; "Snow" in *Poetry*, November 1916. See *The Poetry of Robert Frost*, ed. Edward Connery Lathem (New York: Holt, 1969), p. 543; hereafter cited as RF.
2. Wilfred Gibson, "The Golden Room," in *The Golden Room and Other Poems* (London: Macmillan, 1928), p. 172.
3. See Louis Untermeyer, *Bygones* (New York: Harcourt, 1965), p. 48; and Lawrance Thompson, *Robert Frost: The Years of Triumph* (New York: Holt, 1970), pp. 31, 33–34, 72–75.
4. Theodore Morrison, "The Agitated Heart," *Atlantic*, July 1967, p. 72.
5. Marion Montgomery, "Robert Frost and His Use of Barriers," in *Robert Frost: A Collection of Critical Essays*, ed. James M. Cox (Englewood Cliffs, N.J.: Prentice-Hall, 1962), p. 146.
6. Eban Bass, "Frost's Poetry of Fear," *American Literature*, 43 (1972), p. 604.
7. As reported by Reginald L. Cook, "Robert Frost in Context," in *Frost: Centennial Essays III*, ed. Jac Tharpe (Jackson: Univ. Press of Mississippi, 1978), p. 167.
8. Cook, p. 167.
9. "On Emerson," in *Selected Prose of Robert Frost*, ed. Hyde Cox and Edward Connery Lathem (New York: Holt, 1966), p. 118.
10. Untermeyer, p. 48.
11. John F. Lynen, *The Pastoral Art of Robert Frost* (New Haven: Yale Univ. Press, 1960), p. 33.

12. This item appeared in *The Littleton Courier*, 31 March 1901, with the headline "Sad Tragedy at Bethlehem / Raymond Fitzgerald a Victim of Fatal Accident." It is quoted by Lawrance Thomspon in *Robert Frost: The Early Years* (New York: Holt, 1966), p. 567.

13. John A. Meixner, "Frost Four Years After," *Southern Review*, NS 2 (1966), 876.

14. As reported by Charles H. Foster, "Robert Frost at Bread Loaf," in *Centennial Essays III*, p. 79.

FRANCIS C. BLESSINGTON

"An Old-Type *Natural* Fouled-Up Guy": The Conflicting Voice in Philip Larkin

In "Posterity," a satirical poem in Larkin's latest collection of verse (1974), Jake Balokowsky is writing a biography of Larkin and tells one of his friends:

> "What's he like?
> Christ, I just told you. Oh, you know the thing,
> That crummy textbook stuff from Freshman Psych,
> Not out of kicks or something happening —
> One of those old-type *natural* fouled-up guys."[1]

While it does come out of "something happening," the Larkin voice is an "old-type *natural* fouled-up" one, and these traits help categorize its unresolved conflicts. But critics have sometimes found the reverse. In 1957 Charles Tomlinson found "a tenderly nursed sense of defeat" in Larkin's poems. Later A. Alvarez found him the poet of "gentility," Colin Falck saw him as accepting of the "scientific nightmare," while Donald Davie heard the Larkin voice as "scrupulously neutral": "There is no historical perspective, no measuring of present against past."[2] Indeed, Larkin has found defenders,[3] but they have not pointed to the strong conflicts that lie unresolved but dramatized beneath the smooth veneer.

I

That voice is "old-type" inasmuch as it keeps alive the tradition of a personal, low-key poetry that has maintained a steady place in English literature since the beginning of the nineteenth century. A list of the poets that Larkin himself has written about defines the tradition well enough: William Barnes, Emily Dickinson, Walter de la Mare, Wilfred Owen, Stevie Smith, and John Betjeman, among others. In the introduction to *The North Ship*, Larkin tells us that he has particular interest in Thomas Hardy, whom he acknowledges as a more lasting influence on him than the early Yeats.[4] Relying on this tradition, Larkin uses the resources of formal poetry to grate against our cheap-jack, ephemeral modern world. What Larkin says about the less dramatic poetry of John Betjeman may be said about his own:

> He [Betjeman] addresses himself to his art in the belief that poetry is an emotional business and that rhyme and meter are means of enhancing that emotion, just as in the days when poetry was deemed a kind of supernatural possession.[5]

At times it seems as if the past is scrutinizing the present or a test is being given to experience to see if it can rise out of the commonplace to the level of traditional song, a sort of unearthing of the long-buried poetic roots of our everyday experience:

> Home is so sad. It stays as it was left,
> Shaped to the comfort of the last to go
> As if to win them back. Instead, bereft
> Of anyone to please, it withers so,
> Having no heart to put aside the theft
>
> And turn again to what it started as,
> A joyous shot at how things ought to be,
> Long fallen wide. You can see how it was:
> Look at the pictures and the cutlery.
> The music in the piano stool. That vase.[6]

The iambic pentameter stanzas, rhyming *ababa*, hold the poem above the abyss of sentimentality. The conflict builds when the "old-type" verse form throws a strong metrical accent on trivial words that works against the syntax of the speech. Words like *it, of, if, so, as, how, be, was,* and *in* all receive some metrical stress and sometimes the added stress of rhyme because the trivial details in the old room, some too trivial even to be mentioned, are nonetheless charged with the emotions of loss and failure. The form may be said to represent the past that overcomes the objects in the poem—picture, music, cutlery, even the vase that is frozen alone at the end of the poem because the speaker is struck speechless by the pathos of the scene. Here the meter imitates the trapped-in-time quality that Larkin wishes to impart. The sense of strain in the poem fits the triumph of the past over anything in the present.

Old-type forms can also be used humorously because they can represent simple-minded, even childish, attitudes toward life. The syntactical and the metrical accents coincide to produce a pseudo-doggerel that mocks itself. A good example is the simple-minded professor in "Naturally the Foundation Will Bear Your Expenses" who rushes about the world reading his papers and thinking his little world of pretentious contacts is far more important and adult than the Armistice Day celebration outside the window of the London cab taking him to the airport. The professor is more childish than the patriotic English in his smug pride and name-dropping narrowness. The nursery jingle of the verse undermines his stance and shows him to be the child of foundations:

> — But I outsoar the Thames,
> And dwindle off down Auster
> To greet Professor Lal
> (He once met Morgan Forster),
> My contact and my pal.
> (WW, p. 13)

In "Latest Face," the old-type conflict is generic, a modern piece of Petrarchanism in which the narrator is momentarily enraptured by a passing girl. The title undermines the possibility that this casual occurrence would lead to love, and the poem hints at the impossibility of meeting a Beatrice or a Laura in the modern world, at least for the frustrated narrator in the poem. His misplaced romanticism, transpiring entirely in his own head, leads to a conclusion as forced and ludicrous as it is artificial and dated:

> can
> Denial of you duck and run,
> Stay out of sight and double round,
> Leap from the sun with mask and brand
> And murder and not understand?[7]

Another aspect of the "old-type" conflict appears in the chronological tensions in the poems. A common Larkin approach is to find significance in a piece of the past that has lasted into the present—a photograph, a statue, a place where one was raised or educated, like the room in "Home Is So Sad," or a church, as in his most anthologized and commented-upon poem, "Church Going" (LD, pp. 28–29). In each of these scenes the speaker discovers what, if anything, the past means to the present. The church in "Church Going" is an "accoutred frowsty barn," but it produces an "awkward reverence" in the speaker, who makes offerings to the empty buildings that he often visits trying to comprehend. The church seems to dwarf him and at the same time insist on its own significance, as it sniggers like the whole of the past at the smallness of the present. After the speaker acknowledges the superstitions that organized religion tames and satisfies, he concludes that the church is a memorial to a healthier age, one that celebrated birth, marriage, and death: "what since is found / Only in separation." It represents the dignity of human life itself: "A serious house on serious earth it is."

The poet seems at once to be criticizing and envying the past, as in "MCMXIV" (WW, p. 28), in which he sees in a pre–World War I photograph the innocence that was destroyed in 1914. A similar innocence is enviable in the old statues in "An Arundel Tomb," where the speaker sees with a shock that the earl and the countess are holding hands. The simple-minded purity of the scene strikes the viewer as a quirk of the sculptor, a piece of sentimentality that was as out of place then as now, since love fails to remain ideal. The difficulty of maintaining that peak of affection is imitated throughout the poem by the clash of the stiff short *i, d,* and *t* sounds against the more rounded vowels and liquid consonants:

> Side by side, their faces blurred,
> The earl and countess lie in stone,
> Their proper habits vaguely shown
> As jointed armour, stiffened pleat,
> And that faint hint of the absurd —
> The little dogs under their feet.
> (WW, p. 45)

The stiffness keeps pace with the moaning sounds of loss as the poem continues, because the conflict is unresolved either in poetry or in life.

The old-type voice is not always a modern looking at ancients; we also find Larkin peering out of his own generation at the present and asking the meaning of the present for the past. The present often does not fare very well, as in "High Windows" (HW, p. 17), "This Be the Verse" (HW, p. 30), and "Annus Mirabilis" (HW, p. 34). The so-called sexual revolution of the late sixties is examined in all three poems with humor, irony, and satire. "High Windows" is the most effective of the three, since it parallels the unreflective hopes of the young with the envy of the old, who wish they had led a more hedonistic life when they had the energy and the chance. The last stanza, however, views the whole question from the perspective of the nothingness that surrounds modern man, diminished by endless space and time, and then leaves it to the reader to ask whether semipermanent or merely ephemeral values are best sought after. The "deep blue air" has the alluring promise of happiness and "the sun-comprehending glass" of the high windows implies human understanding and control, such as those of a church, but they are seen as structures that we erect because of the emptiness that surrounds us. Age has brought understanding and perspective to the speaker, who accepts the limits of his life because these limits give it meaning. At the same time, of course, he seeks something permanent that is not there, something beyond the present, which used to be called God. Immediate sexual gratification is not enough for the speaker; he wants something transcendent, beyond the small happiness presented by free love. He does not seem to be able to accept mere sensuality as the purpose of life, any more than the speaker in "The Card-Players" can (HW, p. 23) when he envies their bestial lives but cannot share them. In both poems Larkin presents the traditional conflict of body and soul in a new and refreshing way.

II

Besides these ghosts of the past that spark conflict in Larkin's poetry, we also find a split between the natural and the unnatural. Jake Balokowsky, it will be remembered, underscored the word "natural" in his appraisal of the poet. Many poems represent the difficulties of finding the natural anymore, either in human feelings or in nature. "Myxomatosis" employs a delicate, perverse irony to describe the disease some farmers themselves spread in the early 1950s to wipe out the rabbit population. Ninety-five percent was destroyed, hence there is no mention of a rabbit in the poem:

> Caught in the centre of a soundless field
> While hot inexplicable hours go by
> *What trap is this? Where were its teeth concealed?*
> You seem to ask.
> 　　　I make a sharp reply,
> Then clean my stick. I'm glad I can't explain
> Just in what jaws you were to suppurate:

You may have thought things would come right again
If you could only keep quite still and wait.

(LD, p. 31)

Less strident and more beautiful is "Cut Grass," whose clipped lines
imitate the fallen stalks and whose strong spondaic rhythm imitates the
inevitability of death. In the poem two conflicting forces are at work:
the fertility of nature and the destructiveness of man who cuts down the
stalks before they are dead. The stalks lie, telling their own story in the
blooming June field. Larkin is at his best in this type of indirect lyric
where more is suggested by less:

> Cut grass lies frail:
> Brief is the breath
> Mown stalks exhale.
> Long, long the death
>
> It dies in the white hours
> Of young-leafed June
> With chestnut flowers,
> With hedges snowlike strewn,
>
> White lilac bowed,
> Lost lanes of Queen Anne's lace,
> And that high-builded cloud
> Moving at summer's pace.

(HW, p. 41)

The last few lines move away from the spondaic movement of the
earlier lines because the later lines speak of a still-living part of nature:
the cloud that would nourish the grass if it were still alive, as it should
be if it had lived at nature's pace along with the chestnut flowers and the
white hedgerows. "Lost lanes" may also suggest the eroding of the
English countryside, another of Larkin's themes. The syntax that
interweaves dead and living plants subtly portrays the conflicting scene.

One group of poems shows how unnatural urban life has become. In
"The Large Cool Store," love, like our store-bought commodities, is
"synthetic, new, / And natureless in ecstasies." (WW, p. 30). "Sunny
Prestatyn" (WW, p. 35) and "Essential Beauty" (WW, p. 42) show how
advertising hides the cancers of urban life—sexual frustration, lung
cancer, poverty, and old age—under a gloss of sentimental lies. The
urban wasteland of Larkin's poems is full of "the still sad music of

humanity" that cannot find any relief for its sufferings. In "Here," the speaker speeds from middle-class through working-class to poverty-class neighborhoods to reach the natural freshness of the seaside: "Here is unfenced existence: / Facing the sun, untalkative, out of reach" (WW, p. 9). The freshness he constantly seeks is the message he receives in "The Trees," another of Larkin's successful short lyrics, which concludes with "Last year is dead, they [the trees] seem to say, / Begin afresh, afresh, afresh" (HW, p. 12). While nature insists on replacing the old with the new, such transformation is impossible for those trapped in modern cities. In "The Whitsun Weddings," the June newlyweds are all collected on the train with the narrator and heading towards disappointment as well as the renewal they expect through marriage:

> There we were aimed. And as we raced across
> Bright knots of rail
> Past standing Pullmans, walls of blackened moss
> Came close, and it was nearly done, this frail
> Travelling coincidence; and what it held
> Stood ready to be loosed with all the power
> That being changed can give. We slowed again,
> And as the tightened brakes took hold, there swelled
> A sense of falling, like an arrow-shower
> Sent out of sight, somewhere becoming rain.
>
> (WW, pp. 23)

Readers have pointed to the fertile optimism of the last three lines; no doubt it connects to the squares of wheat to which London's postal districts are compared earlier.[8] Nonetheless, as C. B. Cox has shown,[9] these last lines do not alleviate the conflicting ambiguity in the poem that sees marriage as a "happy funeral" and a "religious wounding." The "sense of falling," "arrow-shower," and "rain" at least continue the undercurrent of futility and the hint of death that also awaits the wedding couples at the end of the journey. Like the poet, we can easily see "it all again in different terms." As Anthony Thwaite said of Larkin's poetry: " 'Wedding-Wind' is the only completely happy poem of Larkin's, the only one in which there is a total acceptance of joy."[10] Yet even that poem ends with a question as to whether that happiness can last (LD, p. 15).

Beneath the stolidity of cities is the emptiness of death, showing through the impersonal ambulances and hospitals, the loneliness that Larkin points out in "The Building" (HW, pp. 24–26). At first the speaker talks of a "kind of nurse," and later of simply "a nurse," as if finally becoming reconciled to where he is. Sometimes the voice in the poem has found the natural, but it is less than heartening.

Such is not the case in "Forget What Did," where the speaker stops writing in his diary because he is presumably becoming too egocentric; henceforth he will write only of larger events outside himself. He will try to make a fresh start:

> Stopping the diary
> Was a stun to memory,
> Was a blank starting.
> (HW, p. 16)

The title emphasizes Larkin's point by dropping out the first-person pronoun. Purging self-pity and egotism, the poem proceeds on a dipodic principle that underscores its theme of getting back to basics. This hammering beat, combined at times with alliteration, sounds the nursery-rhyme, Anglo-Saxon rhythms that derive from the age of *Beowulf* and are at the root of our language. (The four-beat Anglo-Saxon line was later sawed into two.) The thumping double beat and the dangling unaccented syllables that it controls emphasize both the triviality the poet is trying to overcome and the primitive strength he is trying to recapture. The vowel sound of "stun" introduces the new wallop that comes from stopping to think and write about oneself. The overconscious words "cicatrized" and "bleakened" show the depths into which the self-serving style of the poet has led him. Success in poetry is a forgetting of the self, a self that drops out of the last two lines of the poem as they stiffen the verse toward accentual-syllabic meter and give it a strong formality. The subject of his writing will be only "celestial recurrences" that are "observed," anchored in real experience, so that the subjective will have a stabilizing fulcrum. The poet must look at nature with the freshness of actual life, not the repetitiveness of the past. The words in the diary were put there to heal personal wounds and to compensate for loss. That the new resolution is more satisfactory is seen in the masculine ending of the last two lines: "The day the flowers come, / And when the birds go." The dangers to be avoided here are those of a writer who relies on a shy, retiring voice like Larkin's. Nature is the best test for such a voice.

III

In addition to being old-type and *"natural"* Larkin calls himself, through Balokowsky, "fouled-up" as well, a characteristic that qualifies him to comment openly on the fouled-up people that pass through his poems. Ironically Balokowsky is himself trapped in the American college tenure game. He wanted to teach in Tel Aviv but the need for cash and security forced him to settle for college teaching where, if he writes his biography of Larkin, he can get two semesters off to work on Protest Theater. He is in his "cell" at Kennedy Airport lamenting a fate that he unconsciously brought on himself. Another character who lives in a self-imposed cage is "Mr. Bleaney" who lived in the same shabby room "till / They moved him" (WW, p. 10). As the speaker points out, "how we live measures our own nature," although he keeps thinking how narrow Mr. Bleaney's life must have been without realizing that the present tenant of Mr. Bleaney's room, namely himself, is reenacting Mr. Bleaney's life and probably his thoughts. It is easier for him to analyze Mr. Bleaney than to look at himself honestly.

The usual voice in Larkin knows very well, however, that he is "fouled-up," for one of two reasons: either the world is barren or he is.

One group of poems deals with the "fouled-up" childhood: "A Study of Reading Habits" (WW, p. 31), "I Remember, I Remember" (LD, pp. 38–39), "Nursery Tale" (NS, p. 26), and "Send No Money" (WW, p. 43). These poems show childhood as a time of false promises, of romantic delusion and disillusion. "Send No Money" concludes:

> In this way I spent youth,
> Tracing the trite untransferable
> Truss-advertisement, truth.

The childhood poems insist that childhood is so dull and misspent that the sooner it is over the better, as the lambs in "First Sight," who are born in the bleakness of winter, will later learn that there is a warm spring, too (WW, p. 36). That warm spring is the more conscious and controlled world of adulthood, the promise that is metaphorically treated in "Coming," where happiness for a child is beginning to participate in the adult world (LD, p. 17).

"Fouled-up" childhood is often followed by "fouled-up" adulthood, and another series of poems traces the disappointments of marriage: "Afternoons" (WW, p. 44), "The Whitsun Weddings" (WW, pp. 21–23), and "Maiden Name" (LD, p. 23) deal with fallen romantic notions that wither in the winter of the day after. The promises that love makes, like the beautiful blue air of "High Windows," are usually no more than air in Larkin's poetry. In "Sad Steps" (HW, p. 32), an echo of Sidney's thirty-first sonnet, the voice addresses the moon as the traditional "Lozenge of love! Medallion of Art!" The tone is sarcastic, as it was in

Sidney's poem. Both poets lament the impossibility of love's lasting in the world. Sidney wryly asks if love is any better on the moon; for Larkin the moon drifts through the cannon smoke of clouds, a promise of love to the young and naïve but really "high and preposterous and separate." Its generalized sense of alienation is more irredeemable than the alienation in Sidney's Renaissance poem.

Is Larkin then a pessimist? It is true, as Clive James asserts, that he is the "poet of the void,"[11] and, as Anthony Thwaite has commented, that he defines himself by negatives.[12] The complexity of view excludes simple-minded despair, and the aesthetic distance in most of the poems excludes the self-pity that M. L. Rosenthal finds in Larkin.[13] Larkin views this kind of suffering as part of spiritual development, as he says of Thomas Hardy.[14] For Larkin, the poet must tell the truth about where he finds himself:

> Poetry is an affair of sanity, of seeing things as they are. The less a writer's work approximates to this maxim, the less claim he has on the attention of his contemporaries and of posterity.[15]

There is nothing unnecessarily gloomy in this view; his poems are sad

> only insofar as they are about life, and the gloomy thing for everyone is its decline. Things begin bright but end dull. If you couldn't imagine things much better than they are it wouldn't be half so bad. But gloom applied to my poetry is a very silly word. Anyone who looks at death, for instance, and doesn't feel sadness, would have to be an extraordinary person. Once you realize you're going to die you can't see anything else again except in that context.[16]

The pessimism is relieved or at least diluted in various ways. Doubt, for example, helps keep the tension at the end of some poems: how the speaker was struck silent by the sight of "That vase." In "Self's the Man" the speaker, a bachelor, feels superior to henpecked Arnold. But the poem concludes:

> Only I'm a better hand
> At knowing what I can stand
> Without them sending a van —
> Or I suppose I can.
> (WW, p. 25)

In "Reasons for Attendance" the lonely speaker who opts for art concludes his looking in at the possibly happy dancers:

> . . . I stay outside,
> Believing this; and they maul to and fro,
> Believing that; and both are satisfied,
> If no one has misjudged himself. Or lied.
>
> (LD, p. 18)

Humor, noticeable throughout the poetry, also relieves the gloom and puts another face on the incongruities of life. There are also some puns on the poet's name. The pre-World War I Age of Innocence in "MCMXIV" thinks that the war will be "An August Bank Holiday lark." In "Whitsun Weddings" the speaker thinks at first that the wedding parties are "porters larking with the mails," and in "A Study of Reading Habits" (WW, p. 31) the adolescent who identifies with the villains of horror stories finds that "Evil was just my lark." With these devices, Larkin avoids the featherbed of English melancholy.

But being a "fouled-up" voice has its advantages. Where would English poetry be without its conflicts of body and soul, ideal and real, promise and expectation? Being out of sync helps the Larkin voice express the conflicts that make poetry. Larkin says all this and more in "Spring":

> Green-shadowed people sit, or walk in rings,
> Their children finger the awakened grass,
> Calmly a cloud stands, calmly a bird sings,
> And, flashing like a dangled looking-glass,
> Sun lights the balls that bounce, the dogs that bark,
> The branch-arrested mist of leaf, and me,
> Threading my pursed-up way across the park,
> An indigestible sterility.
>
> Spring, of all seasons most gratuitous,
> Is fold of untaught flower, is race of water,
> Is earth's most multiple, excited daughter;
>
> And those she has least use for see her best,
> Their paths grown craven and circuitous,
> Their visions mountain-clear, their needs immodest.
>
> (LD, p. 36)

IV

This voice of "one of those old-type *natural* fouled-up guys" does not stay entirely outside the human dilemma looking in. The conflict in the Larkin voice arises partly because he is an insider too, one of the "guys," as Balokowsky puts it. In his most recent volume, *High Windows* (1974), Larkin is much more at home in the world than he was thirty years before in *The North Ship*, a pattern that Alun R. Jones noticed developing earlier.[17] To see this shift, one need only note the change in emphasis from "those family hols" of the speaker's "unspent" childhood in *The Less Deceived* (pp. 38–39) to the celebration of seaside holidays in *High Windows* (pp. 9–10). The stance is much more social and forgiving now. In "Show Saturday" (HW, pp. 37–39),we find the speaker at a fair. It is a "Grey day for the show but cars jam the narrow lanes." The catalogues of activities give a sense of vitality, whereas similar stanzas in "Here" (WW, p. 9) pile up desolation. The lonely crowd is less lonely now. They come out of their homes to participate unwittingly in a social ritual that the poet blesses in the last line with "Let it always be there." There is a less separated voice here and in "To the Sea." This poem significantly opens the collection:

> To step over the low wall that divides
> Road from concrete walk above the shore
> Brings something back something known long before.
>
> (HW, p. 9)

The voice seems to be rejoining the human chorus. In "Wants," from *The Less Deceived* (p. 22), the speaker discovers that the wish to be alone is beyond all things, beyond the invitation cards, "the printed directions for sex," the family photograph, and the life insurance; but beneath the wish to be alone is the wish to be dead: "Beneath it all, desire of oblivion runs." In the latest collection Larkin acts on this knowledge partly out of human sympathy because helplessness is universal. In "To the Sea" we find "The miniature gaiety of seasides. / Everything crowds under the low horizon." Poetic voice, humanity, and nature seem united under the large umbrella of the seaside sky.

But this reconciliation is intermittent. Like the Saturday fairgoers, the beach crowd decamps. Many of the other poems in *High Windows* try to define the relationship between the voice and the rest of humanity, in contrast to Larkin's earlier impotent envy of the cardplayers' "secret, bestial peace." In "*Vers de Société*," as in "Wants," the invitations come in, but this time the speaker does not end with the river of oblivion but accepts Warlock Williams' invitation in spite of his having to ask "that ass about his fool research" and his sneer at virtue's being "social" (HW, pp. 35–36).

The drudgery of social life is tentatively accepted because of the loneliness that the voice sang of before. The social drudgery is like the dull workaday world that the speaker complains of in a series of poems that stretch through Larkin's career. In the early "I see a girl dragged by the wrists," the poet sees a boy and girl horsing around in the snow and two men shoveling. He has his place with the shovelers, he feels: He does the everyday work. Yet this work is his launching platform for leaps of the spirit:

> Damn all explanatory rhymes!
> To be that girl!—but that's impossible;
> For me the task's to learn the many times
> When I must stoop, and throw a shovelful:
> I must repeat until I live the fact
> That everything's remade
> With shovel and spade;
> That each dull day and each despairing act
>
> Builds up the crags from which the spirit leaps.
>
> (NS, p. 33)

This theme recurs in "Toads" (LD, pp. 32–33) and "Poetry of Departures" (LD, p. 34). In both poems the narrator thinks of and rejects any escape from the "toad" work of everyday life because to live the bohemian life is too artificial and out of touch with ordinary humanity. Perhaps the "toad" work keeps him sane and prepares him for his poetic leaps of spirit. "Toads Revisited" is a portrayal of the commonplace as the imperfect but necessary companion of every human life.

> Walking around in the park
> Should feel better than work:
> The lake, the sunshine,
> The grass to lie on,
>
> Blurred playground noises
> Beyond black-stockinged nurses —
> Not a bad place to be.
> Yet it doesn't suit me,
>
> . . . .
>
> No, give me my in-tray,
> My loaf-haired secretary,

My shall-I-keep-the-call-in-Sir:
What else can I answer,

When the lights come on at four
At the end of another year?
Give me your arm, old toad;
Help me down Cemetery Road.

(WW, pp. 18–19)

The commonplace diction underscored by the music of the verse, the perfect harmony of sound and sense, and the poetry to be found in the most unlikely places show that the Larkin voice can modulate between two keys. He reminds us that what we see every day—tramps shuffling through trash baskets and the switchboard operators—has its poetry too. That everyday occurrences can also sound the note of despair is a mark of Larkin's comprehension and humanity.

By acknowledging the conflicts that it experiences the Larkin voice finds a language "not untrue and not unkind" (WW, p. 29). It finds even desolation worth singing about, which for Larkin is a positive act.[18] Perhaps the positive experience of the conflicts in Larkin's poetry comes out most clearly in "Coming" (LD, p. 17), a poem he included in his edition of *The Oxford Book of Twentieth Century English Verse*. There a child comes upon the Larkin landscape and hears a voice "of adult reconciling," the drawing up of a compromise between opposites, between the voice and its world or between promise and fulfillment, and perceives some pattern to the world, the art traced by the dancer's feet. Indeed the patterned or patterning voice striving for value is the constant value in Larkin's poetry. It makes the child at least start to be happy and keeps "old-type fouled-up"adults sane and writing.

NOTES

1. Philip Larkin, *High Windows* (London: Faber, 1974), p. 27; hereafter cited as HW.
2. Charles Tomlinson, "The Middlebrow Muse," *Essays in Criticism*, 7 (1957), 214; A. Alvarez, in *New Poetry*, rev. ed. (Harmondsworth: Penguin, 1966), pp. 24–25; Colin Falck, "Philip Larkin," in *The Modern Poet: Essays from "The Review"*, ed. Ian Hamilton (London: Macmillan, 1968), p. 108; Donald Davie, *Thomas Hardy and British Poetry* (London: Routledge & Kegan Paul, 1973), p. 65.

3. Three book-length studies have appeared: David Timms, *Philip Larkin* (Edinburgh: Oliver & Boyd, 1973); Lolette Kuby, *An Uncommon Poet for the Common Man* (The Hague: Mouton, 1974); and Bruce Martin, *Philip Larkin* (Boston: G. K. Hall, 1978).

4. Philip Larkin, *The North Ship* (London: Faber, 1945), pp. 9–10; hereafter cited as NS.

5. Philip Larkin, Introd., *Collected Poems*, by John Betjeman, comp. Earl of Birkenhead (Boston: Houghton Mifflin, 1971), pp. xxv–vi.

6. Philip Larkin, *The Whitsun Weddings* (London: Faber, 1964), p. 17; hereafter cited as WW.

7. Philip Larkin, *The Less Deceived* (Yorkshire: Marvell Press, 1955), p. 41; hereafter cited as LD.

8. See, for example, Timms, p. 120; Davie, p. 66.

9. C. B. Cox, "Philip Larkin: Anti-Heroic Poet," *Studies in the Literary Imagination*, 9 (1976), 163.

10. Anthony Thwaite, "The Poetry of Philip Larkin," *Phoenix*, Philip Larkin issue, 11–12 (1973–74), 48.

11. Clive James, "Wolves of Memory," *Encounter*, 42 (1974), 71.

12. Thwaite, p. 57.

13. M. L. Rosenthal, "Tuning in on Albion," *Nation*, 188 (1959) 458–59. See also his *New Poets: American and British Poetry Since World War II* (New York: Oxford Univ. Press, 1967), pp. 23–44.

14. Philip Larkin, "Wanted: Good Hardy Critic," *Critical Quarterly*, 8 (1966), 174–79.

15. Philip Larkin, "Big Victims: Emily Dickinson and Walter de la Mare," *New Statesman*, 77 (1970), 368.

16. John Horder, "Poet on the 8:15" (interview), *Manchester Guardian*, 20 May 1965, p. 9.

17. Alun R. Jones, "The Poetry of Philip Larkin: A Note on Transatlantic Culture" (1962); rpt. *Phoenix*, Philip Larkin issue, 11–12 (1973–74), 149. It is generally agreed by critics and by the poet himself that since *The Less Deceived* (1955) Larkin has not developed much. But see Timms, pp. 93–95, and his "Church Going Revisited: 'The Building' and the Notion of Development in Larkin's Poetry," *Phoenix*, Philip Larkin issue, 11–12 (1973–74), 13–25.

18. See "Raymond Gardner Interviews Dr. Larkin about His Approach to Poetry," *Manchester Guardian*, 31 March 1973, p. 12.

PART THREE

Some Remarks
on Poetry and Criticism

HOWARD BAKER

Salvage

for Samuel French Morse

In random sleights of memory
My past arises—there the field
And boy, and there the wind congealed.
Those days, they ask what elegy?

Once when from pine to hedge the press
Of winter drizzled dusk, I found
An earth-bird feeding, stained with ground,
Stooped close in classic tranquilness.

Once I saw night like chaos rear
From soughing slope to crag; then tame
It cringed at Jupiter's fat flame.
The trees were leaved with tongues of fear.

Or what you said in Normandy
When your calm brow rehearsed my sphere,
"Look how our road has wound up here!"
But gold-bright hair hung over me.

And other places, other lusts,
Taut echoes, salvage from the flood!
Nor yet begrudge the ebbing blood
While gold leaves gleam in Orphic dusts.

ROY HARVEY PEARCE

Poetry and Progress,
Criticism and Culmination:
A Cautionary Tale

I

My role as the teller of this tale is that of a historian of ideas in the Lovejovian mode—that in which I was long ago trained. It will be recalled that the moral of virtually all of Lovejoy's tales is that, properly viewed *ex post facto*, the beliefs and commitments (which together constitute what Lovejoy called "ideas," "idea complexes," and "dialectical motives" of our ancestors may appear not at all ridiculous if understood in their developing intellectual and sociocultural contexts; that, moreover, we might become somewhat self-consciously critical of our own beliefs and commitments (to the point that we may recognize their potential for the ridiculous) through the properly carried-out exercise of relating them in their continuity to those of our ancestors. Lovejoy felt that among his principal "foes" were those *esprits simplistes* who as progressivists were either self-congratulatory or self-flagellating—that is, those who would assure themselves that they were either the inheritors or the victims of an ineluctable idea of progress. This then will be a Lovejovian exercise—with I hope the proper component of irony deriving from a post-Lovejovian's abiding and compulsive sense of human limitations, a sense of the human project as being gloriously tragicòmical.

An epigraph is called for. It follows, Kenneth Burke's poem "Creation Myth":

In the beginning, there was universal Nothing.
Then Nothing said No to itself and thereby began Something.
Which called itself Yes.
Then No and Yes, cohabiting, begat Maybe.

Next all three, in a ménage à trois, begat Guilt.

And Guilt was of many names:
Mine, Thine, Yours, Ours, His, Hers, Its, Theirs—and Order.

In time, things so came to pass
That two of its names, Guilt and Order,
Honoring their great progenitors, Yes, No, and Maybe,
Begat History.

Finally, History fell a-dreaming
And dreamed about Language—

(And that brings us to critics-who-write-critiques-of-
critical-criticism.)[1]

II

Among those whose researches and speculations have led them to conclude that historical process is necessarily progressive, as though it were the result of a "law," there is an overwhelming tendency, regarding poetry (indeed, the arts in general), to come to primitivistic or utopian conclusions. They conclude that poetry (here let "poetry" stand for "literature") was necessarily at its best and most powerful in a time now past, under sociocultural conditions less complex than those that now obtain; or they conclude that poetry will necessarily be at its best and most powerful at some time in the future, under sociocultural conditions more complex than those that now obtain. The speculative historians to whom I refer, let it be said at the outset, were for the most part not primarily concerned with nor interested in poetry. They were if at all only incidentally literary critics or literary historians. Rather, their concern was, in the process of designing a theory of historical development as a mode of progress, to place human institutions—among them poetry in its making—in that development. I want here to instance some key examples of both the primitivistic and the utopian aspects of their researches and speculations and then briefly to inquire into the bearing which all of this might have for our understanding of poetry and the criticism which it entails.

Although there are adumbrations of these notions in classical, medieval, and Renaissance thought, it was during the Enlightenment that they began to take definitive shape. With the coming of the four-stage theory of sociocultural development, particularly in the so-called Scottish Enlightenment, the problem of literature as an institution was systematically confronted. That theory held that society inevitably went through stages of development which were tied to modes of subsistence and that social and cultural institutions were to be comprehended precisely as effects and outcomes of those modes: hunting, pastoral, agricultural, and commercial, to use the favored terms. Movement from one mode to another was taken to be necessary and for the common good, and thus progressive. There were institutions specific to each stage of development, and each institution had virtues integral to it. But the *kinds* of virtues specific to each stage had become progressively better, since complementary to the stage-specific virtues were necessary weaknesses and faults (because also stage-specific). Thus in the earlier stages men, because of the institutional structure of their society, would be particularly courageous, marked above all by personal bravery, and their interpersonal relations would be especially close and spontaneous. On the other hand, at these earlier stages, men would necessarily be cruel, given to warfare; their religion would not be "refined"; they would be incapable of the kind of abstract thinking that made for true philosophizing, higher learning. These latter qualities and capacities of course derived from the institutional structure of societies in the later stages of development, particularly the late agricultural and the commercial stages. There would be no blinking the fact that much had been lost; yet much more had been gained. Among the things that had been—necessarily—lost was the capacity to make great poetry.

Adam Ferguson perhaps best sums up this primitivistic view in his *Essay on the History of Civil Society* (1767). After demonstrating at length that man's sociocultural institutions, as they have derived from developing modes of subsistence, have on the whole improved, he goes on to admit freely that man at the earlier stages of his development produced the best poetry:

> Under the supposed disadvantage of a limited knowledge, and a rude apprehension, the simple poet has impressions that more than compensate the defects of his skill. The best subjects of poetry, the characters of the violent and the brave, the generous and the intrepid, great dangers, trials of fortitude and fidelity, are exhibited within his view, or are delivered in traditions which animate like truth, because they are equally believed. He is not engaged in recalling, like Virgil or Tasso, the sentiments or scenery of an age remote from his own; he needs not be told by the critic, to recollect what another would have thought, or in what manner

> another would have expressed his conception. The simple
> passions, friendship, resentment, and love, are the
> movements of his own mind, and he has no occasion to
> copy.[2]

There is, I emphasize, no desire on Ferguson's part—nor on that of his peers of whom I make him exemplary—to return to that stage of society, and to its institutions, which has made great poetry directly (that is, most powerfully) possible. Writing of that "barbarian" poet Homer in 1735, another Scot, Thomas Blackwell, put the matter succinctly when he expressed his "Wish . . . *That we may never be a proper subject of an Heroic poem.*"[3]

This of course is not the occasion to anthologize such views. Hence I merely instance in addition to the Scots, Vico, Turgot, and Hazlitt, among others, as being, so far as poetry is concerned, primitivists by virtue of being progressivists. But I must cite one other famous instance of a thinker, committed to a theory of historical process at once progressivist and inevitablist, who, for all his admitted sophistication in literary matters, yet held to the primitivistic view:

> A man cannot become a child again, or he becomes childish.
> But does he not find joy in the child's naïveté, and must he
> himself not strive to reproduce its truth at a higher stage?
> Does not the true character of each epoch come alive in the
> nature of its children? Why should not the historic childhood
> of humanity, its most beautiful unfolding, as a stage never to
> return, exercise an eternal charm? There are unruly children
> and precocious children. Many of the old peoples belong in
> this category. The Greeks were not normal children. The
> charm of their art for us is not in contradiction to an
> undeveloped stage of society on which it grew. [It] is its
> result, rather, and is inextricably bound up, rather, with the
> fact that the unripe social conditions under which it arose,
> and could alone rise, can never return.

This of course is Marx in the *Grundrisse.*[4] So much then for my first set of examples of the progressivist as the primitivist.

The utopian view occurs as early as Condorcet's *Sketch for a Historical Picture of the Progress of the Human Mind* (c. 1794). And it occurs in Mill's *System of Logic* (1843). Precisely because it is utopian, it is too generalized to get at in and of itself; for it must exist only as part of a desiderated system. Great poetry will come, we are told. But at this stage, its specific nature and quality can only be generally postulated.

What is important for us, in the context of our immediate concerns, is that great poetry—or perhaps one should say the greatest poetry—cannot be admitted to exist now or to have existed in the past. Thus another progressivist as utopian, Comte, in the *Cours de Philosophie Positive* (1830–42):

> For five centuries, society has been seeking an aesthetic constitution correspondent to its civilization. In the time to come—apart from all consideration of the genius that will arise, which is wholly out of the reach of anticipation —we may see how art must eminently fulfill its chief service, of charming and improving the humblest and the loftiest minds, elevating the one and soothing the other. For this service it must gain much by being fitly incorporated with the social economy, from which it has hitherto been essentially excluded. . . . The most original and popular species of modern art, which forms a preparation for that which is to ensue, has treated of private life, for want of material in public life. But public life will be such as will admit of idealization, for the sense of the good and the true cannot be actively conspicuous without eliciting a sense of the beautiful, and the action of the positive philosophy is in the highest degree favorable to all three. The systematic regeneration of human conceptions must also furnish new philosophical means of aesthetic expansion, secure at once of a noble aim and a steady impulsion. There must certainly be an inexhaustible resource of poetic greatness in the positive conception of man as the supreme head of the economy of nature, which he modifies at will in a spirit of boldness and freedom, within no other limits than those of natural law. . . . What philosophy elaborates, art will propagate and adapt for propagation, and will thus fulfill a higher social office than in its most glorious days of old.[5]

Reading such generalized prose is (as R. P. Blackmur said on a corresponding occasion) like punching a mattress. And I find that I don't get much further when I try to read the utopian remarks about poetry by more recent committed progressivists—specifically Marxists from Trotsky to Marcuse. But that doesn't particularly matter here, since my concern is simply to indicate notions of the fate of poetry and the criticism it entails as they are considered by ideologues of progress when they are in either a primitivistic or a utopian mood.

III

I come then to some recent examples. I wish I could quote them without attribution, because I want to take them as ideal-typical expressions of their sentiments. Let them be at least documents nearly anonymous.

There has developed over the past fifteen years or so a literary movement called ethnopoetics. Its primary impulse is somehow to "recover" those oral poetries which, even if they are part of the written record, have become aesthetically lost to us. Or rather, so the argument goes (and I am persuaded by it), to our own impoverishment we have become lost to them. The movement is, for me, a most important one. It has resulted in the recovery and reexamination of many, many texts, the taping of contemporary oral poetries in the field, and new modes of exegesis and, more important, translation. Inevitably, since much of the material involved comes from the so-called Third World, Marxist critics, with all their progressivist commitments, have dealt with these poetries and have involved themselves in the ethnopoetic movement. Quite naturally indeed, they have tried to define it. A few years ago a large-scale conference on ethnopoetics was held, and some of the papers delivered there were subsequently published in *Alcheringa*, then the movement's main journal.

One of the papers, claiming that the name of the movement should be *socio*poetics, gives this primitivistic account of the place these poetries should play in our lives (italics and capitals are the author's):

> As western man "pacified" New World nature, eliminated
> the "savage," penned them up in reservations, he did the
> same with whole areas of his Being. Indeed, it would be
> difficult to explain the extraordinary nature of his
> (imperialist) ferocity if we did not see that it was, first of all, a
> ferocity also wrought, in psychic terms, upon himself.
> Western man—as defined by the bourgeoisie—restrained
> those areas of Being whose *mode of knowing* could sustain
> the narrative conceptualization . . . of his new world picture,
> but eliminated, penned up on reservations—those areas of
> *cognition* which were, by their mode of knowing, *heretical* to
> the conceptualized orthodoxy that was required. THE MODE OF
> COGNITION THAT WAS PENNED UP WAS A MODE WHICH WESTERN
> MAN (ALL OF US, SINCE IT IS NO LONGER A RACIAL BUT A CULTURAL

TERM) REMAINS AWARE OF ONLY THROUGH POETRY—AND
POETRY AS THE GENERIC TERM FOR ART.[6]

Thus the primitivistic view of poetry by a progressivist critic, which, if
only we allow for differences in rhetoric, has a distinct affiliation with
Ferguson's "The simple passions, friendship, resentment, and love, are
the movements of his own mind, and he has no occasion to copy."

But this progressivist's view is also utopian. For she continues
immediately:

> HENCE IT WOULD SEEM TO ME TO BE THE POINT OF THIS
> CONFERENCE: THE EXPLORATION OF THIS ALTERNATIVE
> MODE OF COGNITION IDEOLOGICALLY SUPPRESSED IN
> OURSELVES, YET STILL A LIVING FORCE AMIDST LARGE MAJORITIES OF
> THE THIRD WORLD PEOPLES. IN THIS COMMON EXPLORATION THERE
> CAN THEN BE NO CONCEPT OF A LIBERAL MISSION TO SAVE
> "PRIMITIVE POETICS" FOR "PRIMITIVE PEOPLES." THE SALVAGING OF
> OURSELVES, THE RECLAMATION OF VAST AREAS OF OUR BEING, IS
> DIALECTICALLY RELATED TO THE DESTRUCTION OF THOSE
> CONDITIONS WHICH BLOCK THE FREE DEVELOPMENT OF THE HUMAN
> POTENTIALITIES OF THE MAJORITY PEOPLES OF THE THIRD WORLD.

A commenter on this paper sums it up, putting the matter in perspective:

> So it is important, that after all of that individualistic
> lyricism there should finally emerge a lyric production that
> reasserts its links to the mainstream of art in human
> societies, and attempts to reinvent that social and collective
> function which poetry and the chanted or spoken or sung
> word have had over all but the most recent centuries of
> human history.[7]

Another primitivistic example, perhaps somewhat more sophisticated than the one I have just related, is Lukács' *Theory of the Novel*,
which has proved somewhat difficult for Marxist critics precisely
because it is not one of Lukács' specifically Marxist treatises. I quote
the summarizing bit of a recent (I take it) Marxist resolution of this
difficulty. What is centrally at issue is Lukács' understanding of
"realism":

> If Lukács' theory of representation is "dogmatic" and
> reductive of the complexity of history and the novel, this

"dogmatism" does not really "originate" in his concept of "historicity" in *The Theory of the Novel* . . ., nor with his conversion to Marxism. . . . Rather the ideal, harmonious presence he attributes to the origin of history in Greece dominates, though not simply and without contradiction, both his early "pre-Marxist," "idealist" work and his later "Marxist," "materialistic" work. The origin of history is never really "lost" for Lukács; for representation is the dialectic at work in fiction to ensure that the presence of harmonious man, that "his" poetry, will be conserved and projected forward onto the end of history. To transform a phrase of Lukács from *The Theory of the Novel*, in this view of history, the historical journey is over as soon as the voyage begins. The presence of harmonious man as the essence of all representation (and interpretation) has put an end to the conflicts, contradictions, and differences of history. Representation in this abstract, dialectical sense *is* the end or the elimination of history.[8]

Only recall the passage from Marx quoted earlier. What is happening here is an appeal (dialectical in good part, as in the statements I have previously quoted, via the diacritical marks) to that idea of *Gemeinschaft*— that is, the primitivist—which is of course at the heart of the passage from Marx: Greek society was genuinely communitarian; modern society is not but could be; poetry is possible only in a *gemeinschaftlich* society. Lukács' notion of realism and the novel can be understood as deriving from a desiderated *Gemeinschaft* precisely as the novel is the modern analogue of the epic. Thus Lukács is even at this stage taken to be Marxist in spite of himself—and, I would add, necessarily a primitivist. The open question remains: Does "the end or the elimination of history" entail the end or the elimination of poetry, of literature? Just as we may devoutly hope that we may never be the subjects of heroic poems, should we hope that we may never be the subjects of novels, the subjects of history? Indeed, can we hope that we may not in any event be *subjects*?

Now some examples of the progressivist as utopian. Here, I must point out, it develops that it is criticism which, having its way with poetry, is culminating. I give three examples, all in the mode that we have been instructed to call structuralist, or poststructuralist, or post-poststructuralist.

There are thus two interpretations of interpretation, of structure, of sign, of freeplay. The one seeks to decipher, dreams of decipherment, a truth or an origin which is free from freeplay and from the order of the sign, and lives like an exile from the necessity of interpretation. The other, which is no longer turned toward the origin, affirms freeplay and tries to pass beyond man and humanism, the name man being the name of that being who, throughout the history of metaphysics and of ontotheology—in other words, through the history of all of his history—has dreamed of full presence, the reassuring foundation, the origin and the end of the game.[9]

There is therefore in every present mode of writing a double postulation: there is the impetus of a break and the impetus of a coming to power, there is the very shape of every revolutionary situation, the fundamental ambiguity of which is that Revolution must of necessity borrow, from what it wants to destroy, the very image of what it wants to possess. Like modern art in its entirety, literary writing carries at the same time the alienation of History and the dream of History; as a Necessity, it testifies to the division of languages which is inseparable from the division of classes; as Freedom, it is the consciousness of this division and the very effort which seeks to surmount it. Feeling permanently guilty of its own solitude, it is nonetheless an imagination eagerly desiring a felicity of words, it hastens towards a dreamed-of language whose freshness, by a kind of ideal anticipation, might portray the perfection of some new Adamic world where language would no longer be alienated. The proliferation of modes of writing brings a new Literature into being insofar as the letter invents its language only in order to be a project: Literature becomes the Utopia of language.[10]

This suggests one final approach to the Text, that of pleasure. I do not know if a hedonistic aesthetic ever existed, but there certainly exists a pleasure associated with the work (at least with certain works). I can enjoy reading and rereading Proust, Flaubert, Balzac, and even—why not?—Alexandre Dumas; but this pleasure, as keen as it may be and even if disengaged from all prejudice, remains partly (unless there has been an exceptional critical effort) a pleasure of consumption. If I can read those authors, I also know that I cannot *rewrite* them (that today, one can no longer write "like that"); that rather depressing knowledge is enough to separate one from the production of those works at the very moment when their remoteness founds one's modernity (for what is "being modern" but the full realization that one cannot begin to write the same works once again). The Text, on the other hand, is linked to enjoyment, to pleasure without separation. Order of the signifier, the Text participates in a social utopia of its own; prior to history, the Text achieves, if not the transparency of social relations, at least the transparency of language relations. It is the space in which no one language has a hold over any other, in which all languages circulate freely.[11]

Were these last three texts taken from a dialogue by Sir Thomas More, I could come directly to grips with them. As it is, I must come indirectly, noting that they seem to be claiming that, once a text is freed from its context (in the language of the last, once a "work" is taken as a "text"), the critic achieves a certain utopian freedom to do as he is pleasured to do, not as the text wills him (often to his displeasure) to do. The subject-object problem at the heart of Western metaphysics and ontology ("ontotheology"?), and thus at the heart of Western criticism, is solved by the elimination (or repression) of the object—this under the guise of getting rid of the bothersome existence of the subject. The critical mode culminates as the critic becomes not the inventor but rather the creator of all he surveys. As with neo-Marxist primitivism, structuralist utopianism issues into a hope for the withering away of literature, as literature no longer consists of more or less stable works by more or less unstable writers but of texts that occasion the celebration of the stability of readers—the role of criticism itself about to wither away.

IV

There is, I think, a lesson (or moral) for us in this tale—however foreshortened my telling has been. I noted at the outset that there was a "tendency" in the progressivist writers whom I have cited to come to primitivistic or utopian conclusions. Let me change "tendency" to "temptation"— and add that the "temptation" has been "yielded to." The temptation derives, I think, from an insistence, an assumption transformed into a principle, that history has a plot. And if there is a plot, there must of course be a beginning, middle, and something corresponding to an end—to say nothing of a series of denouements. Poetry, according to this line of argument, like other sociocultural institutions, must not only be related to and/or derived from collective activities, it must itself be at base a collective activity, an activity whose development can as such be "plotted." And in seeking out evidence of that collective activity and of its plotting, progressivist historians perforce in good part blind themselves to the fact that poetry is made up of poems *qua* poems, of individual statements which, however much they respond to collectively developed modes of expression (that is literary "conventions" or, more fashionably, "mediations"), remain nonetheless individual. I note that in the first place, reading poems (and, I daresay, making them), we are always in the middle, never at a beginning or an end. This is the existential fact that sets historians of poetry their major problem of research, interpretation, and exposition. In the second place, the statements of which poems consist (or which poems make) are fictive—literature being that form of statement in which the capacity of language to make fictions is maximized. This in fact is poetry's—literature's—great use to us: that it allows us to explore to their uttermost *possible* implications the nature of our aspirations, beliefs, and commitments. It allows us indeed to explore them in a myriad series of alternative roles—as we can, in fictions, allow ourselves to imagine ourselves as being other than we are. The progressivist as primitivist or utopian, however, can afford to believe only in the "real"— at most the probable, never the merely possible; his is the way of extrapolation, not imagination. Thus he must locate poetry at that stage in its history when it has appeared, or will appear, to be most real and not at all fictive—most identifiable with the sociocultural actualities in the context of which it has come into being. Since that stage, owing to the fictive nature of poetry, is never now, it must always have been or be yet to come. Thus, necessarily, poetry is discovered to be part and parcel of the collective plot of history.

I conclude—following in the Lovejovian mode—that one test of the ideas of progress is its use, as at least a heuristic device, in enabling us to come directly to grips with the objects (in this case poems) and the subjects (in this case poets and their readers) which constitute the matter it is to organize for us. And surely that idea, should we subscribe to it, would serve only to distance us from poetry and from ourselves as the subjects of poetry, from the very possibility of poetry, from the free and full employment of our knowledge of the languages and the institutions that condition poetry as a means of knowing ourselves for what we have been, what we are, and what we might be. For even though, as I have outlined its various permutations, past and present, it is meant to describe the conditions of the making of poems, inevitably and necessarily it must prescribe the conditions of the reading of poems. In the case of poetry, the irony is that the idea of progress would confine and inhibit, not free, us—both as poets and as readers of poems. After all, primitivism and utopianism in the end as in the beginning derive from our constitutional fear of freedom within finitude. And freedom within finitude in the beginning as in the end constitutes the ultimate condition of poetry.

NOTES

1. Kenneth Burke, *Collected Poems* (Berkeley: Univ. of California Press, 1968), p. 5.
2. Adam Ferguson, *Essay on the History of Civil Society* (1767; rpt. Edinburgh: Edinburgh Univ. Press, 1966), p. 173.
3. Thomas Blackwell, *An Enquiry into the Life and Writings of Homer* (London: n.p., 1735), p. 28.
4. Karl Marx, *Grundrisse*, rpt. trans. Martin Nicolaus (1857; rpt. New York: Random House, 1973), p. 111.
5. Auguste Comte, *Cours de Philosophie Positive*, 6 vols. 1830–1842 trans. Harriet Martineau (London: John Champman, 1953), II, 559–60.
6. Sylvia Winter, "Ethno or Socio Poetics," *Alcheringa*, NS II (1976), 83.
7. Fredric Jameson, "Collective Art in the Age of Cultural Imperialism," *Alcheringa*, NS II (1976), 108.
8. David Carroll, "Representation or the End(s) of History: Dialectics and Fiction," *Yale French Studies*, 59 (1980), 228–29.
9. Jacques Derrida, "Structure, Sign, and Play," in *The Structuralist Controversy*, ed. R. Macksey and E. Donato (Baltimore: Johns Hopkins Press, 1970), pp. 264–65.
10. Roland Barthes, *Writing Degree Zero*, trans. Annette Lavers and Colin Smith (1953; rpt. London: Jonathan Cape, 1967), pp. 93–94.
11. Roland Barthes, "From Work to Text," in *Textual Strategies*, trans. Josué V. Harrari (1971; rpt. Ithaca, N.Y.: Cornell Univ. Press, 1979), pp. 80–81.

WILLIAM MEREDITH

Reasons for Poetry
and the Reason for Criticism

For poetry to become the useful art among us that it has always been in healthy cultures, certain natural generosities must be accorded to it that are now being withheld. Poets must give freely and deliberately the gift of entertainment—accessible, professional, and, above all, attractive entertainment. Readers and listeners must give a quality of attention open to such delight, suspending habitual defenses against an art they may dislike or be ignorant of or even afraid of. The act of generosity required of critics (and this could well deplete their numbers) is selfless appreciation, praise being the essential mode of criticism.[1]

I. The Reasons for Poetry

The Mexican poet José Emilio Pacheco, in a poem called "Dissertation on Poetic Propriety," asks for "a new definition . . . a name, some term or other . . . to avoid the astonishment and rages of those who say, so reasonably, looking at a poem: 'Now this is not poetry.' "[2] I too want to argue for a broader definition of poetry, a definition that will increase our sense of the multitudes that poetry contains. For those of us who care about poetry in this time of widely diverging definitions are apt to be consciously limited in our tastes and churlish in our distates. We often have more precise ideas, based on these distates, about what poetry is not than about what it is.

If I cannot come up with the new definition Pacheco asks for, my comments are at least intended to turn aside the easy negative response in myself and in others to poems that are not immediately congenial. For whenever we say, Now this is not poetry, we are adding to the disuse of all poetry.

Perhaps the most useful definition, in fact, would begin with a statement about expectation: the expectation with which a reader engages a poem and the reasons for which a poet may have undertaken the poem, and the possible discrepancy between the two. Since what is communicated in a work of art is also how it is communicated, a false expectation is almost certain to produce a false reading. Often we confirm this by the happy surprise that comes when a work that had defeated us suddenly opens itself to us—we find that it performs very well the job that was its reason, once we stop asking it to perform some other service that was no part of its intention.

Poems seem to come into being for various and distinct reasons, which vary from poem to poem and from poet to poet. The reason for a poem is apt to be one of the revelations attendant on its making. No surprise in the writer, no surprise in the reader, Frost said.[3] The reason for a new poem is, in some essential, a new reason. This is why poets, in the large Greek sense of *makers,* are crucial to a culture. They respond newly, but in the familiar tribal experience of language, to what new thing befalls the tribe. There seem to be three generic reasons for which poems come into being, but even without these genera the occasion of a poem is always a new thing under the sun.

And poets don't respond as one; they respond in character, with various intuition, to the new experience. What each maker makes is poetry, but why he or she makes it, the reason, is a unique intuition. The reason determines the proper mode of apprehension. It is part of the purpose of every poem to surprise us with our own capacity for change, for a totally new response. Consider David Wagoner's lines called, aggressively, "This Is a Wonderful Poem":

> Come at it carefully, don't trust it, that isn't its right name,
> It's wearing stolen rags, it's never beeen washed, its breath
> Would look moss-green if it were really breathing,
> It won't get out of the way, it stares at you
> Out of eyes burnt gray as the sidewalk,
> Its skin is overcast with colorless dirt,
> It has no distinguishing marks, no I.D. cards,
> It wants something of yours but hasn't decided
> Whether to ask for it or just take it,
> There are no policemen, no friendly neighbors,
> No peacekeeping busybodies to yell for, only this
> Thing standing between you and the place you were headed,
> You have about thirty seconds to get past it, around it,
> Or simply to back away and try to forget it,
> It won't take no for an answer: try hitting it first
> And you'll learn what's trembling in its torn pocket.
> Now, what do you want to do about it?[4]

The resilience such a poem asks of us is a reader's first responsibility. To assume one knows what a poem is going to do is to show the lack of resilience that has kept the poetry public so small in our country and has divided what public there is into dozens of hostile sects. We say our own chosen poetry—olson or Frost, Lowell or Bly—the poetry whose reasons strike us as reasonable, "Now this is poetry," and then generally, of everything else, loudly, airily and with great conviction, "and this is not." Criticism, which is at its most perceptive when most appreciative, is thus often *narrowly* appreciative. It divides and rules and does little to promulgate the astonishment, the larger force of poetry.

It is very easy to reject poems whose reasons do not declare or recommend themselves to us. Take an extreme mode of recent poetry which Robert Pinsky has described in *The Situation of Modern Poetry.* The school, he says, has "a prevalent diction or manner" that embodies, "in language, a host of reservations about language, human reason, and their holds on life." He quotes a poem by W. S. Merwin and says of it:

> "It moves in a resolutely elliptical way from image to
> atomistic image, finally reaching a kind of
> generalization-against-generalizing in the line:
>
> 'Today belongs to few and tomorrow to no one.' "

Pinsky concludes: "This poem presents a style well suited to a certain deeply skeptical or limiting vision of the poetic imagination and its place in the world."[5]

To appreciate a poem conceived in these terms—conceived for what many readers would consider nonreasons—is not easy for most of us. What kind of poem harbors "a host of reservations about language, human reason, and their holds on life" and "with a deeply skeptical or limiting vision of the poetic imagination and its place in the world"? *Aha!* says the part of our mind that waits with a club for *what is not a poem.* How can anything call itself a poem if it mistrusts language and the power of the poetic imagination? Is not all mystery made lucid to the poetic imagination, and precisely in language? But the often ill advised left side of the brain is wrong to thus object. Let us ask it to consider a poem whose last line proclaims this heresy, whose last line in fact is "There are limits to imagination." This is Robert Hass's beautiful "Homeric Simile." It purports to be a simile about how a soldier falls in a certain Japanese movie, and it likens him chiefly to a great pine tree, an image that does not appear in the movie.

Homeric Simile

When the swordsman fell in Kurosawa's *Seven Samurai*
in the gray rain,
in Cinemascope and the Tokugawa dynasty,
he fell straight as a pine, he fell
as Ajax fell in Homer
in chanted dactyls and the tree was so huge
the woodsman returned for two days
to that lucky place before he was done with the sawing
and on the third day he brought his uncle.

They stacked logs in the resinous air,
hacking the small limbs off,
tying those bundles separately.
The slabs near the root
were quartered and still they were awkwardly large;
the logs from midtree they halved:
ten bundles and four great piles of fragrant wood,
moons and quarter moons and half moons
ridged by the saw's tooth.

The woodsman and the old man his uncle
are standing in midforest
on a floor of pine silt and spring mud.
They have stopped working
because they are tired and because
I have imagined no pack animal
or primitive wagon. They are too canny
to call in neighbors and come home
with a few logs after three days' work.
They are waiting for me to do something
or for the overseer of the Great Lord
to come and arrest them.

How patient they are!
The old man smokes a pipe and spits.
The young man is thinking he would be rich
if he were already rich and had a mule.
Ten days of hauling
and on the seventh day they'll probably
be caught, go home empty-handed
or worse. I don't know

> whether they're Japanese or Mycenaean
> and there's nothing I can do.
> The path from here to that village
> is not translated. A hero, dying,
> gives off stillness to the air.
> A man and woman walk from the movies
> to the house in the silence of separate fidelities.
> There are limits to imagination.[6]

At one critical point in the narrative—the simile is offered as a story—
the poet heightens the mystery of metamorphosis by dramatizing the
process itself:

> They have stopped working
> because they are tired and because
> I have imagined no pack animal
> or primitive wagon. . . .
> . . . .
> They are waiting for me to do something
> or for the overseer of the Great Lord
> to come and arrest them.
>
> . . . .
>   I don't know
> whether they're Japanese or Mycenaean
> and there's nothing I can do.

We are asked to believe that the poem takes place at the limits of
imagination, where the poet's debilitating reluctances threaten to
overpower his fancy and drag it back into the territory of the literal. And
the poem shows us, by exhibiting its own process, how the energy is to
be found, in the process of simile itself, to mix modes and times and
feelings in ways that are disturbing and mysterious and, for souls' sakes,
necesary.

I posit three roles a poem may assume, and suggest that in any poem
one of these roles accounts for the stance of the poem. I offer these three
stances not to head off the proper surprise of a new poem but as an
exercise in resilience, the way you might strengthen your eyesight by
looking at objects near, middling, and far in regular succession. I think
of them as three *reasons* for poetry, identifiable genetically with the
DNA impulse that starts a poem growing. The reason behind a poem
shapes its growth and determines the way it is delivered. To stretch the
metaphor further, it determines how the poem is to be picked up and
spanked into breath by the reader.

If every poem is new, it is also associated in its own mind, and ideally in the reader's, with other poems of its species. Poems hold one another in place in our minds, Robert Frost said, the way the stars hold one another in place in the firmament.

The three roles I envision are these:

The poet as dissident. Underlying poems conceived by the poet as dissident is a social criticism, whether of a tyranny, such as George III's or Stalin's, of an abuse, such as nuclear pollution, or of a system, such as capitalism. As an activist poet, the dissident is likely to be formally radical, since the large metaphor of his or her work is revolution, but not necessarily.

The poet as apologist. Poems conceived by the poet as apologist are predicated on acceptance or approval of the human and social predicament of the tribe. However much the poem may focus on errors or imperfections in its subject, an order or decorum is implied in the model. Often the poem's mode is praise, overt or implicit, of the specific subject or of the human condition. Every work of art, the Christian apologist W. H. Auden said, is by its formal nature a gesture of astonishment at that greatest of miracles, the principle of order in the universe. The poet as apologist is apt to have a pronounced sense of form, but not necessarily.

The poet as solitary. While the poem by the poet as solitary will sometimes take the stance of talking to itself, more often it speaks from the poet as individual to the reader as another individual and intends to establish a limited, intense agreement of feeling. There is no implicit agreement about social needs or predicaments. Such solitary experiences—and they make up most of lyric poetry—carry on their backs the world they are concerned with, like itinerant puppet shows. They create a momentary event in which the poet and the reader dwell together in some mutual astonishment of words. The best teacher I ever had told us that a lyric poem can only say one of three things: It can say, Oh the beauty of it, or Oh the pity of it, or it can say, Oh.

The three roles form a crude trinity, and if they are useful at all it is at the elementary level of detecting and dispelling false expectation.

If a poet is committed to an overriding social grievance, as currently some of the best European, Latin American, and U.S. minority writers are, the poem is best read as a kind of ceremonial rite, with a specific purpose. A dissident poem aspires to be an effective ritual for causing change.

If a poet feels, on the other hand (to quote an easygoing character in one of my own poems), that the human predicament "is just a good bind to be in,"[7] the poem should be read as an occasional poem, occasioned by some instance—however flawed or imperfect—of an existing order. An apologist poem aspires to be a celebration.

If a poet thinks of himself or herself only as a man or woman speaking to men and women, the poem should be read simply as a poem. A solitary's poem is a message written on one person's clean slate to be copied on another person's clean slate as an exercise in personhood. A solitary poem wants to become a little universe or a charade.

It is my cheerful illusion that these are fairly clear distinctions to apply to modern poems. Though I apply them to poems, they reflect intentions, brief or long-standing, of the poet who aligns himself with them. They shade into one another, and readers would disagree about many borderline cases. But, at best, they could be helpful in determining how a poem wants to be read.

Terrence Des Pres, a very gifted prose writer, believes that all serious writing today must be politically committed writing, militant writing. Soon after we had debated this for the first time, he put it this way:

> Most Anglo-American poetry (excluding old guys like Milton and Blake) looks at life and says, that's how it is, that's the human condition. Political poetry also says that's how things are, but then, instead of settling for the hard comfort of some "human condition," it goes on to say, this is not how things must be always. Not even death is that final, when you consider that some men are forced to die like dogs, while others have the luck to die human. Political poetry is concerned with precisely this distinction. And if, by way of example, we ardently oppose the designs of state and the powers that be—as, say, during the Viet Nam war years—is this opposition not a true part of our experience? and if so, is it not a fit subject for poems? Fitter, perhaps, than the old laments like lost love, the soul's virginity, etc?

The poem Terrence Des Pres sent with that letter is by the Polish poet Zbigniew Herbert.

Five Men

1

They take them out in the morning
to the stone courtyard
and put them against the wall

five men
two of them very young

the others middle-aged

nothing more
can be said about them

2

when the platoon
level their guns
everything suddenly appears
in the garish light
of obviousness

the yellow wall
the cold blue
the black wire on the wall
instead of a horizon

that is the moment
when the five senses rebel
they would gladly escape
like rats from a sinking ship

before the bullet reaches its destination
the eye will perceive the flight of the projectile
the ear record a steely rustle

the nostrils will be filled with biting smoke
a petal of blood will brush the palate
the touch will shrink and then slacken

now they lie on the ground
covered up to their eyes with shadow
the platoon walks away
their buttons straps
and steel helmets
are more alive
than those lying beside the wall

3

I did not learn this today
I knew it before yesterday

So why have I been writing

unimportant poems on flowers

what did the five talk of
the night before the execution

of prophetic dreams
of an escapade in a brothel
of automobile parts
of a sea voyage
of how when he had spades
he ought not to have opened
of how vodka is best
after wine you get a headache
of girls
of fruit
of life

thus one can use in poetry
names of Greek shepherds
one can attempt to catch the colour of morning sky
write of love
and also
once again
in dead earnest
offer to the betrayed world
a rose[8]

The intention of Herbert's subtle and moving poem seems to be to convert poets from writing the old laments about lost love, the soul's virginity, and so on, and to enlist them in action to change their political circumstances, if not indeed their own political natures. The poem does not simplify. It retains the demanding reticence of poetry. As a conscience, the reader responds, or not, to its call for change, as clear and ambiguous as Rilke's "You must change your life."[9]

Although it is certainly implicit in Herbert's poem that the role of the dissident is the most *urgent* role at a time like ours, I think there is never any deliberate choosing, except on grounds of temperament—the poem's or the poet's—between the three roles. The time is always *a time like ours*. Ours is simply the one we must respond to truly. Each of the three responses I delineate asks a great deal of the writer and the reader. The following short apologist poems don't shirk moral responsibility, rather they contain it within a system whose imperfection they take as given. In Herbert's poem, the imperfections of society can *only* be responded to militantly, by poet and reader. The imperfections in human nature exhibited in the next two poems are sources of grief but lie beyond grievance. They invite various and complex responses.

On Looking for Models

The trees in time
have something else to do
besides their treeing. What is it.
I'm a starving to death
man myself, and thirsty, thirsty
by their fountains but I cannot drink
their mud and sunlight to be whole.
I do not understand these presences
that drink for months
in the dirt, eat light,
and then fast dry in the cold.
They stand it out somehow,
and how, the Botanists will tell me.
It is the "something else" that bothers
me, so I often go back to the forests.[10]

The Whipping

The old woman across the way
    is whipping the boy again
and shouting to the neighborhood
    her goodness and his wrongs.

Wildly he crashes through elephant ears,
    pleads in dusty zinnias,
while she in spite of crippling fat
    pursues and corners him.

She strikes and strikes the shrilly circling
    boy till the stick breaks
in her hand. His tears are rainy weather
    to woundlike memories:

My head gripped in bony vise
    of knees, the writhing struggle

to wrench free, the blows, the fear
worse than blows that hateful

Words could bring, the face that I
no longer knew or loved . . .
Well, it is over now, it is over,
and the boy sobs in his room,

And the woman leans muttering against
a tree, exhausted, purged—
avenged in part for lifelong hidings
she has had to bear.[11]

My third category will probably strike readers as having the same spinelessness as the category "Other" in a quiz or "don't know" in a poll. But in the art that speaks most eloquently for human peculiarity, the poet as solitary seems as serious and deliberate as the socially active or passive poet. The solitary poet is not at odds with either of them but for the moment is removed from them by some concern that can be shared only person to person. Here, then, are two solitary poems.

Keeping Things Whole

In a field
I am the absence
of field.
This is
always the case.
Wherever I am
I am what is missing.

When I walk
I part the air
and always
the air moves in
to fill the spaces
where my body's been.

We all have reasons
for moving.
I move
to keep things whole.[12]

The Bear

Thrown from the boxcar of the train, the bear
rolls over and over. He sits up
rubbing his nose. This must be
some mistake,
         there is no audience here.
He shambles off through the woods.

The forest is veined with trails
he does not know which to follow.
The wind is rising, maple leaves turn up
their silver undersides in agony, there is a
smell in the air, and the lightning strikes.
He climbs a tree to escape. The rain
pours down, the bear is blue as a gall.

                    *

There is not much to eat
in the forest, only berries,
and some small delicious animals
that live in a mound and bite your nose.

                    *

The bear moves sideways through a broom-straw field.
He sees the hunters from the corner of his eye
and is sure they have come to take him back.
To welcome them, (though there is no calliope)
he does his somersaults, and juggles
a fallen log, and something
         tears through his shoulder,
he shambles away in the forest and cries.
Do they not know who he is?

                    *

After a while, he learns to fish, to find
the deep pool and wait for the silver trout.
He learns to keep his paw up for spiderwebs.
There is only one large animal, with trees
on its head, that he cannot scare.

*

> At last he is content to be
> alone in the forest,
> though sometimes he finds a clearing
> and solemnly does his tricks,
> though no one sees.[13]

A poem like Zbigniew Herbert's "Five Men" must necessarily imply that its reasons are the most urgent reasons a poem can have, that other reasons are somehow trivial. Poems themselves are sometimes bullies, or seem to be. But this is true only as one hypothesis precludes another. Poetry has always resisted being used as propaganda simply because, like other fully created things, it contains and rejoices in contradictions. "When you organize one of the contradictory elements out of your work of art," Randall Jarrell tells us, "you are getting rid not just of it, but of the contradictions of which it was a part; and it is the contradictions in works of art which make them able to represent to us—as logical and methodical generalizations cannot—our world and our selves."[14] Contradiction, complexity, mystery—these are not useful qualities in propaganda.

If some of my suggestions about how to open ourselves as readers are valid, they mean that we must be ready to be astonished, even when that is uncomfortable and morally expensive. When we engage a poem we should credit it with infinite options, not just the three that I have labored, which may strike the reader as obvious or incomplete or wrong. Whatever a poem is up to, it requires our trust along with our consent to let it try to change our way of thinking and feeling. Nothing without this risk. I expect hang gliding must be like poetry. Once you get used to it, you can't imagine not wanting the scare of it. But it's more serious than hang gliding. Poetry is the safest known mode of human risk. You risk only staying alive.

II. The Reason for Criticism

I see the chief similarity between criticism and poetry as this: They are truest to themselves when their impulse is generous and catholic. If poetry is accurate praise, then criticism should aspire to be accurate praise of praise. The second part of this essay will introduce two of my own poems, in an immodest attempt to show a similarity between the two forms of praise. It will be anecdotal, when it is not downright chatty.

Long before Randall Jarrell condemned our age, in an essay of that name, as "The Age of Criticism," Robert Frost had said he *never read criticism*. I'm afraid Frost's refusal bespeaks the same exasperated irresponsibility as the New Hampshire woman's well-known remark about elections: "Oh, I never vote. It only encourages them." Frost once said that his idea of good criticism would be for two intelligent friends to sit together over a good book—it was Milton's *Comus* he gave as an example—and let the first reader point to a couple of lines and then pass the book to the second. This friend would read the passage over until he could, with conviction, nod. Then he would find another line or two that were similarly fraught for him and pass the book back. Thus what had been said with genius would be partaken among intelligence.

I take the meaning of this dry parable to be: what can be marveled at in a work of art is marvelous *in its own terms,* and in the manner of Calvinism, either one marvels or one is cast out from marveling. Art resists criticism in the same way it resists paraphrase. The critic, Frost seems to be saying, can only point to a poem, or to a crucial passage in the poem. Many critics are like boring hosts who describe their self-explanatory travel pictures, standing the while between us and the screen or perhaps even between the projector and the screen. It becomes clear that what they are really pointing at is themselves.

"Criticism *does* exist, doesn't it," Randall Jarrell asks, as if to reassure himself that he is among reasonable people, "for the sake of the plays and stories and poems it criticizes?"[15] Making the same assumption, W. H. Auden goes on to tell how the critic can hope to serve the work he addresses.

> What is the function of a critic? So far as I am concerned, he can do me one or more of the following services:
>
> 1) Introduce me to authors or works of which I was hitherto unaware.
>
> 2) Convince me I have undervalued an author or a work because I had not read them carefully enough.
>
> 3) Show me relations between works of different ages and cultures which I should never have seen for myself because I do not know enough and never shall.
>
> 4) Give a "reading" of a work which increases my understanding of it.
>
> 5) Throw light upon the process of artistic "Making."
>
> 6) Throw light upon the relation of art to life, to science, economics, religion, etc.[16]

I have come to love this intimidating definition of criticism because it assumes that the critic and reader, whatever their inequalities, are both looking at the work as if it were more interesting than themselves. This is the way I believe artists look at their work while they are creating it, and the critical insight is bound to profit from approaching the work in the same spirit. One would be embarrassed to say anything so obvious if one were not continually embarrassed by the vanity of criticism.

In the same essay, Auden writes:

> If good literary critics are rarer than good poets or novelists, one reason is the nature of human egoism. A poet or a novelist has to learn to be humble in the face of his subject matter which is life in general. But the subject matter of a critic, before which he has to learn to be humble, is made up of authors, that is to say, of human individuals, and this kind of humility is much more difficult to acquire. It is far easier to say—"Life is more important than anything I can say about it" than to say—"Mr. A's work is more important than anything I can say about it."
>
> Attacking bad books is not only a waste of time but also bad for the character. If I find a book really bad, the only interest I can derive from writing about it has to come from myself, from such display of intelligence, wit and malice as I can contrive. One cannot review a bad book without showing off.
>
> The injunction, "Resist not evil but overcome evil with good" may in many spheres of life be impossible to obey literally, but in the sphere of art it is common sense. Bad art is always with us, but any given work of art is bad in a period way; the particular kind of badness it exhibits will pass away and be succeeded by some other kind. It is unnecessary, therefore, to attack it, because it will perish anyway. . . . The only sensible procedure for a critic is to keep silent about works which he believes to be bad, while at the same time vigorously campaigning for those he believes to be good, especially if they are being neglected or underestimated by the public. . . .
>
> Some books are undeservedly forgotten; none are undeservedly remembered.[17]

The only time Robert Frost spoke to me about my poems was at a luncheon in the dining room of the Westbury Hotel in New York, where neither of us was at home, between (his) trains. What he said was something like this: Your poems are all right, I guess. But you may be getting tired of talking about yourself. It might be a good idea to look at some dramatic poems. There's not enough of that around now. You might want to look at Browning's monologues again, and some of Tennyson's, some of Robinson's. Maybe some of mine. Some things you can say better if you can get someone else to say them for you.

I'd heard him say on another occasion, when someone had mistaken "The Road Not Taken" for a self-portrait, that that poem had been written to tease his shy and indecisive friend Edward Thomas: "Can you imagine *me* saying anything *with a sigh?*"

And once he said, about "Mending Wall," that the neighbor farmer who says "Good fences make good neighbors," rather than the first-person speaker, was himself. "When I say *me* in a poem, it's someone else. When I say somebody else, it might be me."

"Everything written is as good as it is dramatic," he wrote in the introduction to his not very dramatic *A Way Out*,[18] the little one-act play he never allowed to be reprinted.

Soon after our unlikely luncheon, I was working on a poem about atoms. I had been sitting in on a freshman astronomy class and Robert Bless, the very bright instructor, had said simply in passing, that it was fortunate for the human animal that we had been fashioned to the scale we were. If we had been only a thousand times larger, we would be able to triangulate, with our wide-spaced eyes, and would have known from the start, by looking at the stars, that we were insignificant to an unnerving degree. On the other hand, if we'd been made a thousand times smaller, we would be able to see one another's pulsing atomic structure, which might have caused even greater interpersonal mistrust than exists at present.

Well, I was manipulating these data as they affected intelligent, interesting, sensitive, and charming me, and the muse was not warming to our subject. It must have been in an exasperated attempt to use Frost's advice that I gave the poem away. I gave it to a fourteen- year-old high school student, approximately one-third my then age. I put him in Beloit, Wisconsin, where I'd once spent a night. And I made him black. These three mystifications seem to have enabled me to dramatize a mystery which, in my own character, I was only managing to explain away. This is the poem:

Walter Jenks' Bath

These are my legs. I don't have to tell them, legs,
Move up and down or which leg. They are black.

They are made of atoms like everything else,
Miss Berman says. That's the green ceiling
Which on top is the Robinsons' brown floor.
This is Beloit, this is my family's bathroom on the world.
The ceiling is atoms, too, little parts running
Too fast to see. But through them running fast,
Through Audrey Robinson's floor and tub
And the roof and air, if I lived on an atom
Instead of on the world, I would see space.
Through all the little parts, I would see into space.

Outside the air it is all black.
The far apart stars run and shine, no one has to tell them,
Stars, run and shine, or the same who tells my atoms
Run and knock so Walter Jenks, me, will stay hard and real.
And when I stop the atoms go on knocking,
Even if I died the parts would go on spinning,
Alone, like the far stars, not knowing it,
Not knowing they are far apart, or running,
Or minding the black distances between.
This is me knowing, this is what I know.[19]

Robert Frost was generous to me in a number of ways. "Walter Jenks'
Bath" was a critical gift from him, a poem his critical insight enabled me
to find. When the biographical pendulum swings, he will be known as
quite a different man from the one conjured up by the present vogue for
monsters.

He turned to me once when I was traveling to California with
him—turned *on* me, if I wanted to read the body language with which
he delivered the question—and asked, in no context whatever, "You're
not going to write about me, are you?" I replied defensively, as I do now,
"Only to correct error, Robert."

Here are two egregious pieces of error—out of the herd, as egregious
used to mean—of ungenerous criticism that have been roaming the
literary savannahs since Frost died. Before I offer them, I quote civilized
Randall Jarrell again, who incidentally wrote some permanently useful
appreciation of Frost. In the first paragraph of what he terms his
"complaint" against the age of criticism, he said: "I will try to spare
other people's [feelings] by using no names at all." Yet it's interesting
how Jarrell manages to call names anonymously, as it were. His
language seems to rant *ad hominem* when he levels certain charges:

"A great deal of this criticism . . . is not only bad or mediocre, it is *dull*; it is, often, an astonishingly graceless, joyless, humorless, long-winded, niggling, blinkered, methodical, self-important, cliché-ridden, prestige-obsessed, almost autonomous criticism."

Speaking of the way critics look down on the literary insights of creative artists: "In the same way, if a pig wandered up to you during a bacon-judging contest, you would say impatiently, 'Go away, pig! What do you know about bacon?' "

"Many critics are bad, I think, because they have spent their life in card-indexes. . . . If works of art were about card-indexes the critic could prepare himself for them in this way, but as it is he cannot."[20]

We need this kind of name-calling, in which error is turned into allegorical drama. In quoting the following two critical lapses, the two dreadful pieces of slanderous criticism, I hope readers will take them as allegories of the character we can become when we try to write of that which we cannot praise. Like Jarrell, I refrain from identifying the ill-tempered remarks.

The criticism is followed immediately by a poem of mine that intends a kind of appreciation of Frost's life and work. Both the criticism and the poem address the charge of lying. I maintain that in his life and work Frost understood that telling the truth is the difficult name of both games, life and poetry.

It is not that Frost was cold, that he was a tyrant as well as a coward, that he could no more forgive a generous than a selfish act (the former a judgment, the latter a threat), that he treated his friends as if they were enemies and his enemies as if they were himself. No. The shock is that he was from start to finish, and in nearly every aspect of his life, a successful liar. Exposures which to other men might have been the moral lesson and warning of a lifetime were to Frost merely hints that he ought to refine his tactics. To him, age brought only a new birth of vanity, new interests to protect, a thousand new reasons for hoarding all the old deceptions. This makes him terrifying.

Along with Whitman, Dickinson and Stevens, Frost has a place among the greatest of American writers. We know something about the lives of all these poets and they were all isolated souls. Dickinson was fierce in her detachment, Whitman troubled by it, Stevens at perfect ease. Frost is really in a different class: a more hateful human being cannot

have lived who wrote words that moved other human beings
to tears. Filled with hate, and worth hating: after reading
these three careful volumes, one feels that to stand in the
same room with a man about whom one knew a quarter of the
things one now knows about Frost would be more than one
could bear.

In Memory of Robert Frost

Everyone had to know something, and what they said
About that, the thing they'd learned by curious heart,
They said well.
        That was what he wanted to hear,
Something you had done too exactly for words,
Maybe, but too exactly to lie about either.
Compared to such talk, most conversation
Is inadvertent, low-keyed lying.

If he walked in fear of anything, later on
(Except death, which he died with a healthy fear of)
It was that he would misspeak himself. Even his smile
He administered with some care, accurately.
You could not put words in his mouth
And when you quoted him in his presence
There was no chance that he would not contradict you.

Then there were apparent samenesses he would not
Be deceived by. The presidents of things,
Or teachers, braggarts, poets
Might offer themselves in stereotype
But he would insist on paying attention
Until you at least told him an interesting lie.
(That was perhaps your field of special knowledge?)
The only reason to lie, he said, was for a purpose:
To get something you wanted that bad.

I told him a couple—to amuse him,
To get something I wanted, his attention?
More likely, respite from that blinding attention,
More likely, a friendship
I felt I could only get by stealing.

What little I'd learned about flying
Must have sweated my language lean. *I'd respect you
For that if for nothing else,* he said not smiling
The time I told him, thirty-two night landings
On a carrier, or thirty-two night catapult shots—
Whatever it was, true, something I knew.[21]

I have included this poem because I think it makes the point that even very impressionistic and oblique praise can enlighten a subject critically more effectively than the most attentive destructive act can. It is interesting that the two reviewers I quoted were both talking not about the biography purporting to be under review but instead were reviewing the life of the dead man.

To be sure, the critic has a responsibility to define and identify excellence, and this task implies comparative judgments. These, too, are useful to the degree that they are generous. Comparison can be constructive. I conclude with two paragraphs of Jarrell's, in which he wants to praise Whitman's genius for free verse and to compare it with the limiting conventional prosody of one of Whitman's greatest contemporaries, Tennyson. Note the respect and affection—which amount to praise—for Tennyson that emerges from the nice comparison, intended only for the aggrandizement of Whitman. Jarrell has been quoting the *Song of Myself:*

> In the last lines of this quotation Whitman has
> reached—as great writers always reach—a point at which
> criticism seems not only unnecessary but absurd: these lines
> are so good that even admiration feels like insolence, and one
> is ashamed of anything that one can find to say about them.
> How anyone can dismiss or accept patronizingly the man
> who wrote them, I do not understand.
>
> The enormous and apparent advantages of form, of
> omission and selection, of the highest degree of organization,
> are accompanied by important disadvantages—and there are
> far greater works than *Leaves of Grass* to make us realize this.
> But if we compare Whitman with that very beautiful poet
> Alfred Tennyson, the most skillful of all Whitman's
> contemporaries, we are at once aware how much Tennyson
> has had to leave out, even in those discursive poems where he
> is trying to put everything in. Whitman's poems *represent* his
> world and himself much more satisfactorily than Tennyson's

do his. In the past a few poets have both formed and represented, each in the highest degree; but in modern times what controlling, organizing, selecting poet has created a world with as much in it as Whitman's, a world that so plainly *is* the world?[22]

NOTES

1. In the following essay, originally delivered in expanded form as two lectures when I was Poetry Consultant at the Library of Congress, I have avoided discussing the first of these three magnanimities. I have spoken rather about the generosity of mind required of the reader and the critic. The readers and listeners who make up the audience at the Library of Congress, and perhaps the critics who came to the lectures, struck me as being among the saved. But I lectured them all about generosity the way a clergyman will flay the congregation in the pews in front of him for the nonattendance of others. Maybe word of it will get back to the offenders.

2. Jose Emilio Pacheco, *Don't Ask Me How the Time Goes By: Poems, 1964–1968*, trans. Alastair Reid (New York: Columbia Univ. Press, 1978), p. 65.

3. *Selected Prose of Robert Frost*, ed. Hyde Cox and Edward Connery Lathem (New York: Collier, 1968), p. 19.

4. David Wagoner, *Collected Poems, 1956–1976* (Bloomington: Indiana Univ. Press, 1976), p. 221.

5. Robert Pinsky, *The Situation of Modern Poetry* (Princeton: Princeton Univ. Press, 1976), pp. 164–65.

6. Robert Hass, *Praise* (New York: Ecco, 1979), pp. 2–3.

7. William Meredith, *Hazard, the Painter* (New York: Knopf, 1975), p. 17.

8. Zbigniew Herbert, *Selected Poems*, trans. Czeslaw Milosz and Peter Dale Scott (Harmondsworth: Penguin, 1968), pp. 58–60.

9. *Translations from the Poetry of Rainer Maria Rilke*, trans. M. D. Herter Norton (1938; rpt. New York: Norton, 1962), p. 181.

10. Alan Dugan, *Poems 4* (Boston: Little, Brown, 1974), p. 18.

11. Robert Hayden, *Selected Poems* (New York: October House, 1966), p. 54.

12. Mark Strand, *Selected Poems* (New York: Atheneum, 1980), p. 10.

13. David Fisher, *Teachings* (Cotati, Calif.: Back Roads Press, 1977), n. pag.

14. Randall Jarrell, *Poetry and the Age* (New York: Knopf, 1953), p. 128.

15. Jarrell, p. 72.

16. W. H. Auden, *The Dyer's Hand* (New York: Random House, 1962), pp. 8–9.

17. Auden, pp. 8–11.

18. Robert Frost, *A Way Out* (New York: Harbor Press, 1929), p. i.

19. William Meredith, *Earth Walk: New and Selected Poems* (New York: Knopf, 1970), p. 7.

20. Jarrell, pp. 70, 72–73, 74, 89, respectively.

21. *Earth Walk*, pp. 18–19.

22. Jarrell, pp. 127–28.

PART FOUR

Samuel French Morse

WILLIAM BRONK

Backtrack into the Swamp

"What was he looking for, if anything?"

I still go there though I found as you found
the landscape nondescript, devoid of clues.
It's true, Sam, you and I would always go
to look at trees, at flowers and (especially you)
at birds, at any natural thing; I think
though, we never built a special road
to go and look at them. The roads there were
were enough or we took off on our own across
a field or woods not trying to leave a trail
that anyone might follow yet wanting to go
wherever there was that wanted us to go.

We thought it did whether it did or not
and went that way.
                    Now, I'm less sure why.
No, I don't know why the road was there
or the reason even for things that once I thought
important. Some time ago, I started to look
between the trees at empty space. That's what's
important now: the air's vacancy
that hasn't a way or need to be explained.
And, Sam, I think you knew this way back then.

· 147 ·

GUY ROTELLA

"A Certain Doubleness":
The Poetry of Samuel French Morse

In his introduction to Samuel French Morse's first book, *Time of Year*, Wallace Stevens identifies Morse's major subject as "the particulars of experience."[1] This subject, Stevens wrote, defines Morse's "character as a poet," the presence of his "determining personality" in his poems. Forty years and three substantial collections later, the characterization remains precise, for it stresses Morse's consistent attention to the particulars of time, change, and subjectivity. Throughout his career, Morse's poetry has been focused by three versions of that attention, each of them grounded in characteristically exact depictions of those particulars, each of them resulting in a different sort of poem: poems fearful that the facts of time, change, and subjectivity render everything uncertain; poems confident that nature's cyclical constancy and the self's potentially shared imaginings render at least some things certain enough; and poems combining fear and confidence to produce, in Thoreau's phrase, "a certain doubleness."[2]

These ambivalent attentions connect Morse to Stevens, with whom he shares a sure sense of the gulf between mind and object, the desolation of the absurd and alienating incertitude that that gulf creates, and the certain joy in the creation of unifying orders that it requires and allows. In different ways, the same attentions connect him to another master, Robert Frost, with whom he shares a somewhat less than Stevensian subjectivity, a "New Englandly" sort of formal and verbal caginess, and, most pertinent here, the effort to achieve a lasting poise that balances the opposing claims of fearful doubt and faithful confidence. Above all, the various attentions define Morse himself as poet in the world; they mark the distinctive presence of his "determining personality" in his poems.

I

Morse's descriptions of the human and the natural worlds often evoke the facts of time and change that wear away all orders. In "Hardscrabble Farmer," for instance, a man is defeated by a thinness of soil that time uses up. In "Micmac" a remnant Indian in Maine is stunned by the mysteries of change and loss. More typical descriptions are of change in nature, particularly the running down of the seasons, although often such descriptions also include and depict the disappearance of human works. An early poem about the retraction of New England's nine-teenth-century affluence, for instance, concludes its specific narrative with this brooding image of once domesticated land reverting to wilderness:

> The fox runs through the evening like a ghost,
> And night-hawks cry above the ruined shed;
> The well is rank with leaves; the years of dust
> And silence yield the fallen pine its bed.
>
> Only the hunter makes a human noise
> When idle gunning leads his footsteps here
> Where time has sealed the parlor for the bees
> And sunlight burns across the cold frontier.
> ("To Ascend the Mountain," TY, p. 16)

Similar descriptions appear in other Morse poems, including "A Ruined Power Dam" from *The Scattered Causes*[3] and these lines from "The Islands in Summer" in *The Sequences*:

> One house still stands on Jordan, but the rest
> Are cellar holes beside the trickling springs. . . .
> . . . .
> You keep along the shore,
> Looking for derelict, the painted gear
> Some lobsterman has lost, and heaps of shell
> The Abenaki piled there long before
> These others, gone and nameless, settled here,
> Though when they went, or why, you cannot tell.[4]

Such descriptions of time's erosion show that things as they are are in constant flux for Morse, that the world is often a long process of wearing down and wearing out. Morse is thus often a poet of uncertainty.

Moreover, as we will see, this uncertainty is complicated and intensified by his sense of the subjectivity of the self that observes the changing world and by his sense that each self's subjective view may be ultimately its own—alien, private, and difficult, if not impossible, to share. Such ideas inform the passage Morse borrows from Thoreau for the epigraph to his first book. In that passage from "Autumnal Tints," Thoreau indicates his own awareness of subjectivity by asking the reader to imagine the divergent reports on a common scene likely to be produced by consecutive disparate viewers—"a New-England selectman," Julius Caesar, "Immanuel" Swedenborg, and a "Fegee-Islander." The passage continues:

> Or suppose all together, and let them compare notes afterward. Will it appear that they have enjoyed the same prospect? What they will see will be as different as Rome was from Heaven or Hell, or the Fegee Islands. For aught we know, as strange a man as any of these is always at our elbow.[5]

Stevens puts it another way in his introduction to *Time of Year:* "we are not all alike and everything needs expounding all the time." Related to but still more threatened and threatening than those recognitions of subjectivity are these lines from a recent poem by Morse, "The Imaginary Painting": "Everything . . . allows / too much interpretation" (TS, p. 34).

One way Morse attends to the particulars of time, change, and subjectivity, then, is by perceiving the world as a flow of ever-changing specifics and the observing self as separate from that world and from its own observing fellows. Such a view produces his darkest poems. In "The Air Plants" (TY, p. 35), the shifting nature of things both occasions and depicts an anxious insecurity: "For he had felt the world give way / Like sand; and nothing sure of sense / Remained." In another early poem even the aspect of natural change that most promises continuity and pattern, the cyclic alterations of the seasons, turns distressing when snow is expected but the weather warms unseasonably, ironically, and turns to rain:

> After the late rain, the sky brightening,
> Red and gray and bronze, hardly seems good;
> We had expected snow, twice we had felt
> The winter at our backs. Our livelihood,

If somewhat independent of the stars
Is never simple. Men and weather get
Order from four seasons, from night and day:
Men wear this comfort like an amulet,

Proof against sickness of the mortal will;
And weather makes its cycles in a scheme
Easy for men to follow. So, when storms
Turn with the sudden logic of a dream,

We are restless and unsure, fearing a death
We do not understand. And so this rain
Is what we call unseasonable weather,
Brightening autumn grass with a green stain,

A false return. A month now we have watched
The ruffed grouse taking flight over the leaves
In the back woods, known elementary frost
Where we have hunted. But the rain deceives,

Burdening us with mist against the will,
And a late sky, warm with unlooked-for rose;
Summer was too long past, like the ripe fall,
And we expected cold and the deep snows.

("End of a Year," TY, p. 44)

The best treatment of these matters in *Time of Year* is in "The Track into the Swamp." Friends explore a local "wilderness" in which they find an abandoned track that ends in "scrub and shadow" where nature takes it back. Thus the facts of change are invoked again, but here they are less threatening; some knowledge might "explain" the persistence of a swamp within a township or the failure of whatever enterprise occasioned the lost road, as science can explain a "summer snow." The poem's real mystery, then, is not so much these occurrences as the unknown, unknowable subjective selves of the man who made the track and of those who come to follow and wonder at it:

What was he looking for, if anything?

He took the longest way to learn
What sedge and grasses thrust
From crumbling ice the glacier left;

> Where sundew, like a burning glass,
> Lies open to the light.
> Whatever was apparent here
> He must have seen,
> Though deeper in the swamp, perhaps some trace
> Of time before the Pleistocene still shows.
> What conscious aim he had
> Remains as secret as our own.
>
> (p. 23)

The threats of the fluid world and the subjective self continue to provide an important focus for Morse's poems in subsequent volumes, as in these passages from the five-part sequence "The Mirroring Mind":

> our self-reproach obscures
> The shifting images in black and white
> That are the world, and only what they are.
>
> (SC, p. 30)

> Perhaps the silver giving back the light
> Inside the mind is not a trick at all.
> The world reversed and left confused with right
> (Till right is wrong?) astonish and appall
> Our common sense . . . .
>
> (SC, p. 29)

In "A Kind of View," even unmediated perception is brought up short by limitation:

> I look one way from the porch, as far
> As the summer light and the crowding trees —
> As much as a couple of hundred yards —
> Allow the eye; though for all it sees
>
> One way, straight forward, it misses much.[6]

Related but more desperate boundaries are the subject of part III of "Then, Now, Hereafter," a meditation on the failures of experience and language to organize sequential particulars, including the self, into connected, that is, related and meaningful, patterns:

> Hereafter is the sign, the ampersand
> Between this present and the time to come,

> For what we are or may be when we stand
> Where we can look back here. Struck blind or dumb
> By what we were—by what we really are—
> We should not think it might be otherwise.
> We shall not even know how long or far
> It was, nor how we got there. Mere surmise
> Must fill the gap between the now and then:
> A feint of light, some half-remembered talk,
> A gesture out of context, nameless men
> And indecisive wars, a broken lock;
> The odds and ends of time we knew before.
> *And* by itself means *and*, but nothing more.
>
> (TC, p. 18)

At times, as in "Footnote to a Revolution," it is precisely our attention to the particulars on which generalization must be based that prevents our attempts to generalize: "We see too much of time and place / To know the world for what it is" (TC, p.45). In "Coming Back," the very self that sees time and place alters and is lost, and even memory "brings us almost face to face" with only "what we were, not what we are" (TC, p. 57). In "Primum Mobile," the self hopes again to perceive particulars, those of fading summer, and to perceive them well enough to achieve a lasting abstraction; again it fails:

> A few of us who sit up late
> To listen for some outward pause
> Before the season ends, will wait,
> We think, till time becomes pure cause.
>
> The last house, now, puts out its light,
> And the sky clears. If, now and then,
> We catch the sounds of nature right,
> We lose them. We are lonely men.
>
> (TC, p. 85)

Similar themes persist in Morse's most recent work. In part V of "The Islands in Summer," the world's change is located not in the world but in the always altering self:

> I know the spot,
> And I can take you there. If it should seem
> Much changed from what you knew, it is the same.

> All that is different is what you forgot.
> Nothing is really altered but the name—
> "Sweetwater"—that is just an old man's dream.
>
> (TS, p. 6)

Change and loss, and the implication of the present in them, are the subjects of a poem on the extinction of the once wondrously populous passenger pigeon and of the primitive, gentle tribe of Beothuks:

> A host, said Audubon, you too might hear
> above the golden treetops all day long,
> with music in their wings—but they were gone
> by Sarajevo, more than twenty years
> before your time.
>
> They were familiar here,
> Grenfell recalled, till they were set upon —
> a gentle-spoken tribe whose only wrong
> was to have blessed the strangers with their spears
> to welcome them: as heedless as the birds,
> and hunted much the same.
>
> If once again,
> we court extinction, though the morning sky
> looks clear enough, we ought to know the words
> for quarry and for hunters flown so high
> they never see their prey—*like birds, like men.*
>
> ("Passenger Pigeons, Beothuks, You," TS, p. 23)

A related sense of humanity's transient insignificance appears in part IV of "Recognitions," where the only human artifact visible from even so intimate a vantage as the moon is the shadowy thread of the Chinese "emperor's Wall" (TS, p. 42).

Similarly, the artifacts humans make in attempting to hold and capture change, to stop it, are undercut by the insufficiencies of the makers themselves, their forcings of pattern and failures of inclusion, as in the last line of "A Woodcut in a Book": "The frame defines as much as you can know" (TS, p. 24). Collaterally, after describing the contents of a photograph of travelers in Japan, "Not in the Picture" goes on to describe the facts and mysteries that elude containment in such frames: "What you cannot see" (TS, p. 30).

The desolation produced by change and loss and by the subjective self's unbreachable limits receives most potent expression in the bleakness of "Off Shore":

> The ice that pushed and jostled with the tide
> all afternoon still whispers in the slack
> beyond the jetty.
>
> Only flashers mark
> the channel now.
>
> The ghosting seiners lie
> in milder latitudes, so far outside
> the town's uncertain life no reach or tack
> will ever bring them in.
>
> It is too dark,
> too late to keep a watch; and if the sky
> brings out the schooling winter stars, you will
> not sleep the sounder for their being there.
>
> They swim too deep for any net you cast.
>
> Your Banks are all fished out.
>
> (TS, p. 29)

Such is aging, lonely man in a fluid world.

II

In most of the passages quoted so far, only uncertainty is certain. Everything runs down and away; the result is sometimes something like despair. However, if Morse shares with Stevens the awareness of shifting particulars, of the permanent gulfs between self and object and between the self and other selves, he also shares with him the joy this circumstance permits. For it is precisely change and subjectivity that allow each man, however constrained, to make and make again his own connections, orders, patterns, and relations, to make meaning, to make a world. This brings us to the second, more typical way Morse attends to the facts of time, change, and subjectivity: he affirms nature's constancy and the power of imagination to order life's chronic and random events in significant sequence, and he also affirms the possibility that such imaginings might be shared, even held in common, with others (he does this more confidently than Stevens, as his frequent use of plural pronouns shows). The affirming aspect of Morse's art has, of course, already been implied. The quotations from Thoreau, Stevens, and Morse grouped above and repeated here (what four different men will see in a common scene "will be as different as Rome was from Heaven or Hell, or the Fegee Islands"; "we are not all alike and everything needs expounding all the time"; "Everything allows / too much interpretation") suggest affirmative as well as negative responses, for they indicate our freedom from a single or final view. Furthermore, Morse's formal proclivities also suggest his hope of ordering: he writes occasional villanelles and sestinas, frequent sonnets, even more frequent quatrains and other regular stanzas; most of his poems are rhymed, most employ iambic meters. In fact, several of the poems already quoted are turned toward affirmation before they end. At any rate, more common in Morse's work than poems despairing of the place of subjective consciousness in an altering world are poems that assert and celebrate the power of consciousness to give shape, briefly or not, to that world, and so to itself.

The strongest indication in *Time of Year* that these confidences stem from the ordering powers of craft and art appears in "The Birthday Party and the Fire: A Record." The youthful speaker has watched an old man permit, even help, his barn burn to the ground. The old man's equanimity mystifies the speaker, who almost wonders if the farmer had set the blaze himself. Sensing the question, the old man suggests it *could* have been lightning. The poem ends with the speaker's recognition of the human need for and joy in the controlled growth of reconstruction— that which keeps us alive: "All the vivid fall / You worked to clear the wreckage of the fire; / And afterwards, rebuilt, to your desire" (p. 34).

"An Intervale" shows that eroding change can become the very stuff of stability. In the crucial stanza, process permits, rather than revokes, possession:

> So love, as much as living, keeps us here;
> We have them both to keep, as we have time,
> Acknowledging the weather and the change
> Our livelihood depends on, in our love,
> To notice how the changes keep us home.
>
> (SC, p. 36)

Several other poems in *The Scattered Causes* achieve related certainties through friendship, love, and imagination, among them "A Garland of

Snow for Christmas," "Late April," "For New Year's, 1951," and "A Winter's Dream." Consider, too, the final passage of "A New Atlantis":

> We do not show
>
> Our change to all the outer dark,
> But keep this power within us, sweet
> As the pure noon we recollect
> When shadow gathered at our feet
>
> And the world's wholeness came to flood.
> We saw the drowning country blurred
> Like some Atlantis out of time,
> Unchanged but somehow faintly stirred
>
> In the grave distance we could span,
> Until the vision focussed there:
> The lowland lay beneath us, clear
> Through all its depth of summer air.
>
> We cannot say how we have kept
> Our certitude, as we have done,
> But since that day we live at peace
> In a new country of the sun.
> (pp. 61–62)

Faith in the ordering power of imagination is an explicit subject in several poems of Morse's third collection, *The Changes*. "Thoreau" pays tribute to the transcendentalist's constant effort to know and create what lasts; "He knows / Some meaning will endure." Stevens' creative ordering of the "mere objectiveness of things" is celebrated in the imitative compliments of " 'The Poet Who Lived with His Words' ":

> You loved the morning always. . . .
> . . . .
> The air as clear as change composing sight
> To your identity, the light seen through
> To the pure words of it, imagined, true.
>
> (p. 39)

And: "You spoke of change like something that the mind / Could cling to in the light. . . . The day became the world." And: "A metaphor

imagined, improvised / Words of the thing, you said, were what de-
vised / The day. . . . The day became a radiance of thought." "The Gold
of Troy" asserts the human constancy of such creations.

The way creative "play" can turn random specifics to significant
patterns is the concern of two poems involving Morse's son. In "Sam's
Picture," father and son collaborate on a commonplace sort of drawing:
"a house," "a row of little trees," a "hill, a pond"; their skill is not great:
"I cannot even draw a line / That's straight enough to be a roof"; "the
pond / Looks like an egg." Still, the result is miraculous. They share
their made-up world: "I draw a boy, not much like you, / Beside the
pond. 'That must be me.' " Their common recognitions justify belief:
"You make the world as bright and new / As Adam's knowledge; and for
me, / You make imagination true" (pp. 62–63). "The Game" has a
similar theme. On a trip north, father and son play an alphabet game
and, in the process, imagination's exercise joins their separate selves in
mutual comprehension. This is the poem's conclusion (the boy speaks
first): "'We're here. We made good time— / For all this way, I mean.' /
And I know what you mean" (p. 70).

As its title suggests, *The Sequences* contains many poems in which
the "particulars of experience" take on meaningful shapes, the use of
sequences itself suggesting relations beyond "particulars." At times the
source of meaningful shape is nature's continuity and man's imaginative perception of it, as in "The Whitethroat in July":

> Over, over and over, clear
> And unmistakable as when
> We thought we heard it first, we hear
> The whitethroat call, and call again:
>
> Two notes, then three, intent and sweet,
> Then three notes after, after, till
> Across the meadow they repeat
> As faintly as an echo will,
>
> The sequences.
> (p. 3)

Similar continuities and perceptions mark the sequence "Myriads."
The following is from the eleventh of its twelve sections:

> Now all along the streets, the green
> flares up again.

. . . .
You can feel the ground
under your feet; and in your hands
the sunlight sweetens flesh and bone.

You can believe the world is round.
(p. 17)

"The Perseids" section of the "Recognitions" sequence also makes the point, redeeming at least in part a bleaker fact:

their orbit seems defined,
and whether we are here
to wonder at their light,
they will be back next year.
(p. 41)

Shape in other poems of *The Sequences* is more explicitly produced by ordering imagination. In "A Miniature," for instance, a Persian artist's skill is such that the fictive permanence of his painting of a prince's tiger hunt comes "true" beyond the facts of process and change:

In the known world, far seems far; and near,
In its perspective, would give the lie
to the spellbound hunt.

But the painter knew:
nothing could change the blue of the sky,
the hover of the glittering spear.

The tiger leaps.

And the fiction is true.
(p. 28)

In "It Is to Sound," music redefines the world "according to no logic but its own." It propounds a "symmetry," an "order" that, "though a commonplace / familiar as your pulse," is able to "endue / the world with eloquence beyond all praise" (p. 26).

III

So far, we have seen Morse as attending to the facts of time, change, and subjectivity in two ways: sometimes he feels that change and subjectivity render everything uncertain; at other times he feels that nature's repetitions, the self's imaginings, and the possibility of sharing those imaginings can permit permanence and form. However, Morse's "determining personality" is most present in his poems when those first two sorts of attention work together, and that is his third kind of attention: it is then (in the larger shapes of his books and his career as well as in specific poems) that his "certain doubleness" becomes most clear.

As mentioned above, Morse's doubleness, the grief and joy that arise from the world's flux and the self's subjective state, connect his work to Stevens'. Just as surely the typical mode of Morse's "duplicity" shows important differences between them. In a typical Stevens poem, the shape, much simplified, of doubleness is something like this: the poet-speaker perceives resemblance in the world of flux; an act of imagination then builds that resemblance into an orderly pattern, creating a world; then, as the poet-speaker realizes that the perception of resemblance was subjective and the act of imagination a fictive imposition at a remove from the real, the orderly pattern, the created world, collapses, or its collapse is predicted or implied. It will be clear that Morse's poems involve such elements. However, in a representative Morse poem, those elements do not come together in the rising-falling pattern typical of Stevens. Instead, their patterns are closer to those of Frost: the poems contain the conflicting claims of doubt and belief, skepticism and faith in difficult balance. We have seen those claims unbalance in Morse to produce fine poems, but at his best he joins them to achieve a poised and "certain doubleness."

Such patterns are fairly rare in *Time of Year*, where most poems are given over to either certainty or doubt. There are, however, hints of what is to come, as in the awareness in "Problem of Knowledge" that the cost of the gain of growth is time and death, or the inclusive sense of possibility and limit (flower and snake) in these lines from "The Adder's Tongues": "This is your place, as near as you will get / To simple peace" (p. 20). There are further indications in the assent to complexities of weather in "New England Summer" and in the judgments and mercies of "Alexander Wilson: The Birds."

The indications do not reach what they point to until *The Scattered Causes*. In that volume balance between hope and despair is frequently attained. "For Reason, War" evokes humanity's long, repetitive history of violence, destruction, and waste. The result is recognition but not defeat. The poem's close is an ambivalent array:

> So the mind's grief
> Will change. But what

> The heart may ask
> Is its relief:
> The little love
> Beyond belief.
>   (p. 23)

Is the "little love / Beyond belief" the delusion of wishful thinking, or does it assert the existence of redeeming possibility? What remain are affirmation and qualification, claim and counterclaim.

In "The Circus," balance is subject as well as result. The circus is presented as an "archetype" for humanity's hope, for something beyond the facts of time and death. Such hope is naïve ("only what / The children hope"); nonetheless, we need it. The poem turns to affirmation at its end:

> And all a man
>   Can ever do
> Must answer then
>   For love and hope,
> As the girl climbs
>   The fraying rope.
>   (p. 27)

As it turns, however, qualification persists: "all a man / Can . . . do" seems less than all; "Must answer . . . / For," at best, is making do; the rope, whatever lifeline, frays. Man, like the acrobat, must take the rope, knowing it is frayed, and climb it nonetheless. Related ambiguities temper section III of "The Mirroring Mind," in which the power of visionary imagination to set the world to rights is at once affirmed and doubted ("if," "may," "dream," "distrust"):

> Perhaps the silver giving back the light
> Inside the mind is not a trick at all.
> The world reversed and left confused with right
> (Till right is wrong?) astonish and appall
> Our common sense; but if our inner sight
> Can show us anything, we may recall
> A dream of Eden, still remote and bright,
> Which we distrust, like Adam in his fall.
>   (p. 29)

Such poems of inclusion and balance are apt to be even better when they are grounded in Morse's typically precise depictions of natural detail and event. "The Northern Summer" portrays a self able to give "unstinting praise" to the beauty of the day but, on the same day, to accept "without surprise / The ditches rank with goldenrod and weeds / On a hot, dusty summer afternoon" (p. 35). In "Toward Harvest," imagined timelessness and the constant fact of time interpenetrate and comment on each other:

> Making our late world whole, we grow to see
> Apples like fat October in a tree
> Still green and perfect on its darkening bole
> As the round fruit it bears: for round is whole.
>
> The scent of apples waxes with the moon
> And longer nights; and often, now, at noon
> The simple sunlight slants like falling frost
> Across the orchard. Nothing yet is lost;
>
> Though apples bend the branches to the ground.
> They ripen still. The world grows truly round.
> Only when one warm Northern Spy lets go
> Are we aware of change to come, like snow.
>
> (p. 48)

Most of the closing section of *The Scattered Causes* is made up of poems for Morse's wife, Jane. The plural pronouns rightly suggest that most of these are poems of certainty and love, but some also contain Morse's "certain doubleness." In both "The Deer at Indiantown" and "A Memory of Trees," love and imagination create moments of timeless perfection, but the limits of such acts ("too bright") are recognized as their achievement is claimed. "A Memory of Trees" concludes:

> . . . the only world we see
>
> Is what imagination makes too bright:
> The past we keep, the dream . . . until we turn,
> Acknowledging our love, to see the room
> Like a late Northern orchard, all afire
> With the slow sweetness of its sudden bloom.
>
> (p. 60)

Related attainments of balance distinguish *The Changes*, as in "Above the Snow Line":

At sixteen thousand feet the butterflies
Blow in a yellow cloud across the snow,
An effigy of sunlight you must prize,
The dream beyond discovery, as though
     The pure surmise,

Made visible at last, could stay your mind:
Science is fact, and fact is what the world
May come to be, still true but undefined
Like loneliness. These golden insects whirled
     Benumbed and blind,

Too frail to stem the currents of the air
Lifting them to the reaches of the last
Cold passages of ice, die in the glare
Of light on light, as in the frozen past.
     But you are there.

     (p. 19)

The crucial line expressing the poem's tension is its last. Fact surely overcomes the dream; nevertheless, human presence may enable the creation of an "effigy," the dream "Made visible at last." Or perhaps a companion makes the loss bearable.

The four sections of "Star Poems" also qualify and assert humanity's quest to make the ideal real. The conclusion of part II provides an apt example:

All matter changes shape,
And though the light will grow,
Substance cannot escape,

Become pure form, unless
The body and the mind
Achieve the very thing
For which they were designed.

     (p. 43)

The "very thing" is perfection, of course, and at the same time death, perfection's price. Again, a tensioned balance is the result. Similarly, in "The Poem" the threat of randomness and the human hope for wholeness and form are beautifully poised:

Not what the world must mean, but what it is.
As if you held all summer in your hand
Like dripping pebbles picked up from the sea's
Drowned bottom, with a single golden strand

Of weed the color of the August light
Under the surface, clinging like the cold
To your wet fingers; substance not so bright
In the thin air. No one can safely hold

Much in so little, in so little much,
For long, or whole. Whatever runs between
Your fingers may be lost, but still you touch
The fragments of the world, for what they mean.

(p. 90)

In *The Sequences* Morse's "certain doubleness" about the self in the world continues to be drawn from distinct and distinctive specifics. The affirmations and negations that doubleness suggests often occur in larger units than in previous volumes: in the sections of sequences as well as in parts of poems. Even brief examples show the continuing presence of Morse's "determining" self. Imagination's potent art and delusive artifice is again a subject in the first poem of the sonnet sequence "The Islands in Summer." The human raising of chance particulars to significant shape is at once asserted and called in question:

"A kind of constellation when the light
Is rare enough, and you can see as far
Down east as this," you say, "the islands are,
Of several magnitudes, though none so bright
As Deneb or Arcturus on a night
Moonless and black, without a cloud to mar
Its depth, so clear the least imposing star
In Cygnus or Boötes shines out white.
Ironbound, Jordan, Yellow, Heron, Stave,
Calf, Preble, Dram . . ." You link them one by one
Into the figure of a giant brave
Asleep in Frenchman Bay, though you must know
The islands need the great daystar, the sun,
To be made out even in fancy so.

(p. 4)

Other examples can be briefer still. In "Myriads," part IX, the speaker acknowledges the mixture of clarity and chaos in even the clearest moment, the unseen building of change in what seems a visible changelessness: "The day's too clear / not to be a weather breeder" (p. 15). In part XI of the same sequence, the changing light of coming spring "Between the budding elms" "expands / the limits of the world as known," but the confident hope this asserts is qualified as the latter line roves over: "the light expands / the limits of the world as known / a little" (p. 17). Expands "a little"; is known "a little." The last line of the poem is also complex: "You can believe the world is round." "[C]an believe" affirms the imagination's leap from known fact to general truth (after all, the world *is* round); it also suggests contradictions in the ambiguities of "believe" and in the "but" that "*can* believe" implies. More direct balances appear in part II of "Recognitions": " 'There is the world,' we said, 'maybe for good— /or ill, maybe' " (p. 40). Part IV of "Recognitions" exposes the vanity of humanity's view of its "mastering" self-importance. "From the moon" "the one / real artifact visible," the one particular of human self-assertion to be seen, is "a single black thread in the sun's / empty glare, a shadow so long / it must be that emperor's Wall" (p. 42). Distance, like time, reduces all to insignificance. Nevertheless, the poem, still carefully qualified, concludes with real and modified faith:

> though it may prove
> delusive in terms of worth,
> there is much to say for the view
> (as a view) of the earth from earth.
> (p. 43)

In its precise and precisely balanced recognitions of possibilities and limits, there is much, too, to say for Morse's "determining" view of the earth from earth.

In his introduction to *Time of Year*, Wallace Stevens suggested that Morse's poems would have that quality of "moral beauty" Lionello Venturi attributes to Cézanne. They do have it: the moral beauty of selection and precision, of the refusal of easy affirmation or easy despair, of the effort to know and to tell the "certain doubleness" of truth. As Stevens elsewhere says, in slightly different words, accurate observation equals accurate thought. He might have added accurate belief.

NOTES

1. Wallace Stevens, Introd., *Time of Year* by Samuel French Morse (Cummington, Mass.: Cummington Press, 1943), p. viii; hereafter cited as TY.
2. Henry David Thoreau, *Walden*, ed. J. Lyndon Shanley (Princeton: Princeton Univ. Press, 1971), p. 135. Morse uses the passage containing this phrase as an epigraph to *The Sequences* (Boston: The Poets at Northeastern Series, 1978).
3. Samuel French Morse, *The Scattered Causes* (Denver: Swallow, 1955); hereafter cited as SC.
4. *The Sequences*, p. 5; hereafter cited as TS.
5. Henry David Thoreau, *Excursions and Poems*, Vol. V of *The Writings of Henry David Thoreau* (Boston: Houghton Mifflin, 1906), p. 287.
6. Samuel French Morse, *The Changes* (Denver: Swallow, 1964), p. 9; hereafter cited as TC.

SAMUEL FRENCH MORSE

From "Beach Glass"

The loomings in July
are all we really know
about antipodes.
We watch them come and go

until we seem to see
those nameless atolls where
the palms grow upside down
and marlin swim in air.

But if we acquiesce
at times to such a view,
it isn't one we'd want
to grow accustomed to.

We like the commonplace
of sea and spruce too much
to be impressed by some
mirage we cannot touch,

though substance also is
illusion of a kind,
and what we call the world
has yet to be defined.

SAMUEL FRENCH MORSE

A Candle for Advent

Make no mistake, the world is cold.
Advent is long and difficult,
For all its promise. We must hold
The dark at bay against the odds
Of doubt and ignorance with one
White candle now for warmth and sun.

So small a light cannot dispel
The bitter frost for long nor keep
Us warm enough to keep us well.
The fragile wax consumes like hope.
But it is all we have to stay
The numbness of our black dismay.

And we survive, somehow, the chill
Despite ourselves. We go our ways
In the dead dark alone until
The greater light is there to touch
Our fear, and warm us from afar.
Our candle blossoms like the Star.

The Contributors

HOWARD BAKER is a novelist, poet, critic, and playwright. His work appears in the *Oxford Book of American Verse*.

FRANCIS C. BLESSINGTON teaches at Northeastern University. He is the author of *Paradise Lost and the Classical Epic* (Routledge & Kegan Paul, 1979).

PETER BRAZEAU is the author of a forthcoming oral biography of Wallace Stevens, *Parts of a World: Wallace Stevens' Connecticut Years Remembered* (Random House).

WILLIAM BRONK is a poet and essayist. His collected poems, *Life Supports* (Elizabeth Press and North Point Press, 1981), won the American Book Award for poetry.

ROBERT BUTTEL teaches at Temple University. He is the author of *Wallace Stevens: The Making of Harmonium* (Princeton, 1967), as well as a book on Seamus Heaney.

BONNIE COSTELLO teaches at Boston University. Her *Marianne Moore: Imaginary Possessions* has recently been published by Harvard University Press.

FRANK DOGGETT is a critic. Among his books are *Wallace Stevens: Poetry as Thought* (Johns Hopkins, 1966) and *Wallace Stevens: The Making of the Poem* (Johns Hopkins, 1980).

RICHARD EBERHART's latest book of poems is *Ways of Light* (Oxford, 1980). Oxford will publish a new collection of his poems, *The Long Reach*, in 1983.

Contributors

DOROTHY EMERSON was the poetry editor of *Scholastic Magazine* from 1933 to 1940. Her most recent poems have appeared in *Poetry* and *The Yale Review*.

WILLIAM MEREDITH is the author of seven collections of verse, among them *Earthwalk: New and Selected Poems* (Knopf, 1975) and *The Cheer* (Knopf, 1980). He is currently Henry B. Plant Professor of English at Connecticut College.

SAMUAL FRENCH MORSE is a poet, scholar, and critic. He has published four collections of his own poems and a biography of Stevens, *Wallace Stevens: Poetry as Life* (Pegasus, 1970), and he has edited *Poems of Wallace Stevens* (Vintage, 1959) and *Opus Posthumous:Poems, Plays, Prose by Wallace Stevens* (Knopf, 1957).

ROY HARVEY PEARCE teaches at the University of California, San Diego. He is the author of *The Continuity of American Poetry* (Princeton, 1961), *The Savages of America* (new ed., Johns Hopkins, 1965), *Historicism Once More* (Princeton, 1969), and is a general editor of the Centenary Edition of the works of Nathaniel Hawthorne.

GUY ROTELLA teaches at Northeastern University. He is the author of *E.E. Cummings: A Reference Guide* (G. K. Hall, 1979). His *Three Contemporary Poets of New England: William Meredith, Philip Booth, and Peter Davison* will soon be published by G. K. Hall.

JOHN SEARS teaches at Vassar College. He has published essays on Frost, Hawthorne, Timothy Dwight, Theodore Dwight, Jr., and the landscape of Mauch Chunk, Pennsylvania.

WILLIAM STAFFORD's books include *Stories That Could Be True: New and Collected Poems* (Harper & Row, 1977). A new collection of his poetry, *A Glass Face in the Rain*, was published by Harper & Row in 1982.

ROBERT PENN WARREN's most recent book is *Rumor Verified: Peoms 1979–1980* (Random House, 1981).

Index

A

Aeneas, 43, 46
Aiken, Conrad, 4
Althouse, Howard, 46
Alvarez, A., 93
Anchises, 46
Asch, Barbara, 70
Auden, W. H., 129, 137–138
Audubon, John James, 154

B

Bacon, Sir Francis, 66
Barlow, Joel, "Advice To A Raven in Russia," 6
Barnes, William, 94
Bass, Eban, 84
Beecher family, 6
Berger, Arthur, "Ideas of Order," 4
Berkeley, Bishop, 8
Betjeman, John, 94
Blackmur, R. P., 116
Blackwell, Thomas, 115
Blake, William, 53, 130
Bless, Robert, 139
Bly, Robert, 126
Bogan, Louise, 4
Brinnin, John Malcolm, 4
Browning, Robert, 139
Burke, Kenneth, "Creation Myth," 112–113

C

Caesar, Julius, 150
Caillois, Roger, 31
Campbell, Dr., 47
Cézanne, Paul, 165
Church, Barbara, 7, 21
Church, Henry, 9, 17, 21
Comte, Auguste, Cours de Philosophie Positive, 116
Condorcet, Antoine-Nicholas de, Sketch for a Historical Picture of the Human Mind, 115
Cook, Reginald, 86
Corot, Jean Baptiste Camille, 21
Cox, C. B., 99

D

Dailey, W. N. P., 47
de la Mare, Walter, 94
Des Pres, Terrence, 130
Deutsch, Babette, 4
Dickinson, Emily, 94, 141
Driver, Clive E., 65, 81
Dufy, Raoul, 14
Dugan, Alan, "On Looking for Models," 133

E

Eberhart, Richard, 4
Eliot, T. S., 4, 13
Emerson, Ralph Waldo, 86

F

Falck, Colin, 93
Feo, José Rodríguez, 21, 22
Ferguson, Adam, Essay on the History of Civil Society, 114–115, 118
Fisher, David, "The Bear," 135–136
Fitzgerald, Raymond Tracy, 90
Flint, Cudworth, 4
Four Saints in Three Acts, 9
Frost, Robert, 5, 9, 82–92, 125, 126, 129, 137, 138, 139, 140, 141–142, 148, 160; "The Bonfire," 87; "Brown's Descent," 82; "Desert Places," 87; "Design," 87, 89; "The Fear," 85, 87; "The Gum Gatherer," 82; "The Hill Wife," 87; "Love and a Question," 85; "A Masque of Mercy," 84; "A Masque of Reason," 84; "Mending Wall," 82, 85, 87, 139; Mountain Interval, 82; "An Old Man's Winter Night," 87; "Out, Out—," 82–83, 87–91; "The Road Not Taken," 139; "Snow," 82–87, 91; "The Sound of Trees," 82; "Tree At My Window," 86; "The Vanishing Red," 82; A Way Out, 139

G

Garrigue, Jean, 74, 75, 81
George III, King, 129

Geyzel, Leonard van, 18
Gibson, Wilfred, "The Golden Room," 83
Gray, Thomas, "Sonnet on the Death of Richard West," 6
Grenfell, Wilfred, 154

H

Hall, Donald, 64
Hals, Franz, 18
Hardy, Thomas, 94, 102
Hartford Wits, The, 6
Hartmann, Geoffrey, 51
Hass, Robert, "Homeric Simile," 126–127
Hayden, Robert, "The Whipping," 133–134
Hazlitt, William, 115
Herbert, Zbigniew, "Five Men," 130–133, 136
Homer, 115, 127
Hooker, Thomas, 6
Humphreys, David, "Sonnet . . . Addressed To My Friends At Yale College, On My Leaving Them To Join The Army," 6

J

James, Clive, 102
James, Henry, 79
Jarrell, Randall, 136, 137, 140–41, 143–144
Jobbins, Emma, 47
Jones, Alan R., 104

K

Klee, Paul, 14
Knopf, Alfred A., 4
Kreymborg, Alfred, 4, 65

L

Landor, Walter Savage, 51
Larkin, Philip, 93–107; "Afternoons," 101; "Annus Mirabilis," 96; "An Arundel Tomb," 96; "The Building," 99–100; "The Card-Players," 97, 104; "Church Going," 96; "Coming," 101, 106; "Cut Grass," 98; "Essential Beauty," 98; "First Sight," 101; "Forget What Did," 100; "Here," 99, 104; "High Windows," 96, 97, 101; *High Windows,* 104; "Home is so Sad," 94–95, 96, 102; "I Remember, I Remember," 101; "I see a girl dragged by the wrists," 105; "The

Large Cool Store," 98; "Latest Face," 95; *The Less Deceived,* 104; "Maiden Name," 101; "Mr. Bleaney," 101; "Myxomatosis," 97–98; "Naturally the Foundation Will Bear Your Expenses," 95; "MCMXIV," 96, 103; *The North Ship,* 94, 104; "Nursery Tale," 101; "Poetry of Departures," 105; "Posterity," 93, 97, 100–101, 103–104, 106; "Reasons for Attendance," 103; "Sad Steps," 101; "Self's the Man," 102; "Send No Money," 101; "Show Saturday," 104; "Spring," 103; "A Study of Reading Habits," 101, 103; "Sunny Prestatyn," 98; "This Be the Verse," 96; "To the Sea," 104; "Toads," 105; "Toads Revisited," 105–106; "The Trees," 99; *"Vers de Société,"* 104–105; "Wants," 104; "Wedding Wind," 99; "The Whitsun Weddings," 99, 101, 103
Latimer, Ronald Lane, 26, 69
Laughlin, James, 81
Lear, King, 53
Lewis, Sinclair, 6
Litz, A. Walton, xiii, xiv
Lovejoy, Arthur O., 112
Lowell, Robert, 126
Lukács, Georg, *Theory of the Novel,* 118–119
Lynen, John F., 89

M

MacLeish, Archibald, 4
Marcuse, Herbert, 116
Marx, Karl, *Grundrisse,* 115, 119
McAlmon, Robert, 65
Meixner, John, 91
Meredith, William (as subject), "In Memory of Robert Frost," 142–143; "Walter Jenks' Bath," 139–140
Merwin, W. S., 126
Michelangelo, 53
Mill, John Stuart, *System of Logic,* 115
Milton, John, 130; *Comus,* 137
Monroe, Harriet, 8, 9
Montgomery, Marion, 84
Moore, Marianne, 4, 64–81; "In the Days of Prismatic Color," 67; "The Jerboa," 69; "An Octopus," 69; "The Plumet Basilisk," 69; "Roses Only," 73–77;

Selected Poems, 68; "Things Others
Never Notice," 69; "Those Various
Scalpels," 77–79
More, Sir Thomas, 121
Morrison, Theodore, 83
Morse, Jane (wife), 162
Morse, Samuel French (as subject), xiii, xiv,
148–166; "Above the Snow Line," 162–
163; "The Adder's Tongues," 160; "The
Air Plants," 150; "Alexander Wilson:
The Birds," 160; "Beach Glass," 167;
"The Birthday Party and the Fire: A
Record," 156; "A Candle for Advent,"
169; *The Changes*, 157, 162; "The
Circus," 161; "Coming Back," 153;
"The Deer at Indiantown," 162; "End of
the Year," 150; "Footnote to a Revolu-
tion," 153; "For New Year's 1951," 157;
"For Reason, War," 160; "The Game,"
158; "A Garland of Snow for Christmas," 156– 157; "The Gold of Troy,"
158; "Hardscrabble Farmer," 149; "The
Imaginary Painting," 150; "An Intervale," 156; "The Islands in Summer,"
149, 153–154, 164–165; "It is to
Sound," 159; "A Kind of View," 152;
"Late April," 157; "A Memory of Trees,"
162; "Micmac," 149; "A Miniature,"
159; "The Mirroring Mind," 152, 161;
"Myriads," 158–159,165; "A New Atlantis," 157; "New England Summer,"
160; "The Northern Summer," 162;
"Not in the Picture," 154; "Off Shore,"
155; "Passenger Pigeons, Beothuks,
You," 154; "The Poem," 163– 164; "The
Poet Who Lived With His Words," 157–
158; "Primum Mobile," 153; "Problem
of Knowledge," 160; "Recognitions,"
154, 159, 165; "A Ruined Power Dam,"
149; "Sam's Picture," 158; *The Scattered Causes*, 149, 156, 160, 162; *The
Sequences*, 149, 158, 159, 164; "Star
Poems," 163; "Then, Now, Hereafter,"
152–153; "Thoreau," 157; *Time of Year*,
148, 150, 151, 156, 160, 165; "To Ascend
the Mountain," 149; "Toward Harvest,"
162; "The Track into the Swamp,"
151–152; "The Whitethroat in July,"
158; "A Winter's Dream," 157; "A
Woodcut in a Book," 154

Morse, Samuel French, Jr., 158

O

Olmsted, Frederick Law, 6
Olson, Charles, 126
Owen, Wilfred, 94

P

Pacheco, José Emilio, "Dissertation on
Poetic Propriety," 124
Pinsky, Robert, *The Situation of Poetry*,
126
Pound, Ezra, 21

R

Resnais, Alain, *Providence*, 58–59
Rilke, Rainer Maria, 132
Robinson, Edwin Arlington, 139
Roney, Lila James, 42, 43, 47

S

Santayana, George, 55–56
Sauer, Eleanor, 46
Sauer, John C., 47
Seasongood, Murray, 5
Shakespeare, William, *Macbeth*, 91
Sidney, Sir Philip, 101–102
Sigourney, Lydia Huntley, 6
Simons, Hi, 10, 17, 21
Smith, Stevie, 94
Stalin, Josif, 129
Stein, Gertrude, 69
Steinmetz, Mary Owen, 43
Stevens, Benjamin (grandfather), 41
Stevens, Elizabeth (sister), 37, 38,39, 40, 43
Stevens, Elizabeth Barcalow (grand-
mother), 41
Stevens, Elsie (wife), 9, 19, 41
Stevens, Garrett (brother), 38, 41
Stevens, Holly (daughter), 47
Stevens, John (brother), 37, 38, 39, 40, 41,
47
Stevens, Mary Catherine (sister), 47
Stevens, Wallace, xiii–xv, 4–59, 68, 69, 70,
81, 141, 148, 150, 155, 156, 157, 160, 165;
"Adagia," xiii, 4; "Anything is Beautiful
If You Say It Is," 15; "As You Leave the
Room," 53–54; "The Auroras of
Autumn," 20, 28, 49; "The Bed of Old
John Zeller," 43–46; "The Comedian as

the Letter C," xiii, 26; "A Clear Day and No Memories," 24; "The Common Life," 14; "A Completely New Set of Objects," 19; "Connoisseur of Chaos," 15, 36; "Credences of Summer," 20, 49; "Debris of Life and Mind," 20; "Extracts from Addresses to the Academy of Fine Ideas," 28; "Farewell to Florida," 12; "Ghosts as Cocoons," 32–34; "The Glass of Water," 15; *Harmonium*, 11, 17, 81; "How to Live. What to Do," 26, 27–28, 29; "The Idea of Order at Key West," 8, 59; *Ideas of Order*, 13, 26, 29; "In a Bad Time," 58; "July Mountain," 54; "The Latest Freed Man," 16; "Like Decorations in a Nigger Cemetery," 13; "Lions in Sweden," 13; "Long and Sluggish Lines," 54; "Looking Across the Fields and Watching the Birds Fly," 59; "The Mechanical Optimist," 12–13; "The Man on the Dump," 16; "The Man Whose Pharynx Was Bad," 7; "The Man with the Blue Guitar," 10; "Le Monocle de Mon Oncle," 26; "The Motive for Metaphor," xiii–xiv, 49, 50; "Mrs. Alfred Uraguy," 29; "Mystic Garden & Middling Beast," 13; *The Necessary Angel*, 8, 10–11, 12, 23, 32; "The News and the Weather," 31; "The Noble Rider and the Sound of Words," 30, 32; "Not Ideas about the Thing but the Thing Itself," 4, 56; *Notes Toward A Supreme Fiction*, 13, 16–17, 18, 26, 30; "Of Hartford in a Purple Light," 14; " On the Way to the Bus," 58; "An Ordinary Evening in New Haven," 20, 27, 50; "Outside of Wedlock," 42–43, 46; "The Owl in the Sarcophagus," 56; "Owl's Clover," 30–31; *Parts of a World*, 13, 14, 16, 17, 29; "The Plain Sense of Things," 23–24; "The Planet on the Table," 58; "The Pleasures of Merely Circulating," 34–36; "The Poems of Our Climate," 14; "A Primitive like an Orb," 22; "Prologues to What Is Possible," 50, 54–55; "A Quiet Normal Life," 49; "Recitation After Dinner," 42, 43; "The River of Rivers in Connecticut," 50; "The Rock," 4, 20; "The Sail of Ulysses," 50; "Sailing after Lunch," 9; "Some Friends from Pascagoula," 28, 29–30, 31–32; "Sunday Morning," 26; "Three Travelers Watch a Sunrise," 8, 19; "To an Old Philosopher in Rome," 20, 55, 56; "What We See Is What We Think," 22

Stone, Samuel, 6
Strand, Mark, "Keeping Things Whole," 134
Swedenborg, Emanuel, 150
Sweeney, John L., 4

T

Tasso, Torquato, 114
Tennyson, Alfred Lord, 139, 143
Thayer, Scofield, 68
Thomas, Edward, 139
Thoreau, Henry David, 148, 156, 157; "Autumnal Tints," 150
Thwaite, Anthony, 99, 102
Timon of Athens, 53
Tomlinson, Charles, 93
Trotsky, Leon, 116
Turgot, Anne-Robert-Jacques, 115
Twain, Mark, 6

U

Untermeyer, Louis, 87

V

Venturi, Lionello, 165
Vico, 115
Vidal, M., 21
Virgil, 46, 114

W

Wagoner, David, "This Is a Wonderful Poem," 125–126
Waller, Edmund, "Go, Lovely Rose," 75
Watson, J. S., 68
Webster, Noah, 6
Whitehead, Alfred North, xiii
Whitman, Walt, 141, 143–144; *Leaves of Grass*, 143; *Song of Myself*, 143
Wilbur, Richard, 4
Wilder, Thorton, 19
Williams, William Carlos, 4, 15–16, 64–81; *Al Que Quiere*, 65, 81; *An Early Martyr*, 69; *Kora in Hell*, 65, 67, 71; "Marianne Moore," 67–68; *Paterson*,

70; "Portrait of a Lady," 79–80; "The Rose," 71–73, 76; *Spring and All*, 67, 68, 71–73, 80

Wilson, Jane MacFarland (Wallace Stevens' niece), 37, 38

Wordsworth, William, 6; "Composed Upon Westminister Bridge," 14

Y

Yeats, William Butler, 48–59, 94; "An Acre of Grass," 53; "After Long Silence," 48; "The Apparitions," 52, 55–56; "Beautiful Lofty Things," 52; "Byzantium," 51;

"The Circus Animals' Desertion," 53; "A Dialogue of Self and Soul," 48; "Lapis Lazuli," 48–49, 56; *Last Poems*, 52; "Long-legged Fly," 50; "The Municipal Gallery Revisited," 52; "Sailing to Byzantium," 51; "The Spur," 53; "The Statesman's Holiday," 56–57; "Under Ben Bulben," 52; "Vacillation," 48, 49, 51; "Why Should Not Old Men Be Mad," 52

Z

Zarathustra, 22